The White Rose and the Swastika

Adrian Flynn

OXFORD
UNIVERSITY PRESS

OXFORD
UNIVERSITY PRESS

Great Clarendon Street, Oxford OX2 6DP

Oxford University Press is a department of the University of Oxford.
It furthers the University's objective of excellence in research,
scholarship, and education by publishing worldwide in

Oxford New York

Auckland Cape Town Dar es Salaam Hong Kong Karachi
Kuala Lumpur Madrid Melbourne Mexico City Nairobi
New Delhi Shanghai Taipei Toronto

With offices in

Argentina Austria Brazil Chile Czech Republic France Greece
Guatemala Hungary Italy Japan Poland Portugal Singapore
South Korea Switzerland Thailand Turkey Ukraine Vietnam

Oxford is a registered trade mark of Oxford University Press
in the UK and in certain other countries

British Library Cataloguing in Publication Data

Data available

ISBN: 978 019 832102 6

MIX
Paper from
responsible sources
FSC® C007785

Typeset by Fakenham Photosetting Limited

Printed in Great Britain by Bell and Bain Ltd, Glasgow

Acknowledgements

Extract from *Sophie Scholl and the White Rose* by Annette Dumbach and
Jud Newborn (Oneworld Publications, 2006), first published as *Shattering
the German Night* (1986), text copyright © Annette Dumbach and Jud
Newborn 1986, 2006, reprinted by permission of the publishers.

Artwork by Neil Chapman/Beehive Illustration.
Photo of the White Rose Monument is Wikimedia/Oxford University
Press.

Cover images: Bettmann/Corbis; iStock Photo; Photodisc/Oxford
University Press

The Publisher would like to thank Jenny Roberts for writing the
Activities section.

Contents

General Introduction

With a fresh, modern look, this classroom-friendly series boasts an exciting range of authors – from Pratchett to Chaucer – whose works have been expertly adapted by such well-known and popular writers as Philip Pullman and David Calcutt.

Many teachers use OXFORD *Playscripts* to study the format, style, and structure of playscripts with their students; for speaking and listening assignments; to initiate discussion of relevant issues in class; to cover Drama as part of the curriculum; as an introduction to the novel of the same title; and to introduce the less able or willing to pre-1914 literature.

At the back of each OXFORD *Playscript*, you will find a brand new Activity section, which not only addresses the points above, but also features close text analysis, and activities that provide support for underachieving readers and act as a springboard for personal writing.

Many schools will simply read through the play in class with no staging at all, and the Activity sections have been written with this in mind, with individual activities ranging from debates and designing campaign posters to writing extra scenes or converting parts of the original novels into playscript form.

For those of you, however, who do wish to take to the stage, each OXFORD *Playscript* also features 'A Note on Staging' – a section dedicated to suggesting ways of staging the play, as well as examining the props and sets you may wish to use.

Above all, we hope you will enjoy using OXFORD *Playscripts*, be it on the stage or in the classroom.

What the Author says

There's an unusual monument outside Munich University in Germany: a cluster of leaflets scattered on the pavement. It's only when you know the story of the students who started a resistance movement against Hitler and his ruling Nazi government there during the Second World War, that the monument makes sense.

The group of students called itself 'The White Rose' and was centred around a brother and sister, Hans and Sophie Scholl. In many ways the members of the White Rose were very ordinary. Like most students they enjoyed having a good time with friends. They fell in and out of love. They liked travelling and all had high hopes for the future. But they also had the courage to resist what they thought was great evil, no matter how dangerous it was to do so in such times.

The play covers a period of 10 years in the lives of Hans and Sophie. To make it both readable and performable, many of the people they knew and events they experienced have had to be omitted. For this reason, not all the members of the Scholl family are mentioned. A number of the less central members of the White Rose are also left out, as are some of the friends Hans and Sophie made who deeply influenced their thinking. Their omission isn't a judgement on the value of what they did; it's simply to keep the cast size manageable, and the story comprehensible within the dramatic time-frame.

Occasionally, too, the sequence of events in the play is different from what actually happened. For instance, in real life Hans had his argument with a Hitler Youth leader after he'd been to the Nuremberg Rally, not before. For stage purposes, however, it seemed to work better the other way round. The dialogue throughout the play is invented, although it is all based on accounts of the lives of the White Rose members.

The events portrayed are also all based in fact. Even the slightly ludicrous costume acquired by Johann Reichhart throughout the course of the play is an accurate reflection of what someone in his position would have worn at the time.

My main aim in writing 'The White Rose' is to prompt the reader to learn a little more about this very ordinary, and yet remarkable, set of young people. If the play also raises the question, 'What would I have done in their place?', it will definitely have done its job.

The play has been researched from a variety of sources. *The White Rose*, written by Inge Scholl and published by the Wesleyan University Press, is a valuable fund of information, especially on the Scholls' family life. *A Noble Treason* by Richard Hanser, published by G.P. Putnam's Sons, New York, gives a full and gripping account of the White Rose group, and its historical context. *At the Heart of the White Rose* is a collection of extracts and diary entries written by Hans and Sophie, which is edited by Inge Jens and published by Harper and Row. There is also a very useful chapter in Anton Gill's *An Honourable Defeat* published by Henry Holt. Anyone wanting to know more about the group might also enjoy reading *Sophie Scholl and the White Rose* by Annette Dumbach and Jud Newborn, published by Oneworld Oxford. A German film on the subject was made in 2005 by Marc Rothemund. The English version is entitled 'Sophie Scholl'. There are also a number of useful websites one can explore for further information, simply by putting 'The White Rose' into a search engine.

A Note on Staging

The Stage

The action of 'The White Rose' should be continuous, with no breaks for scene changes, except where a blackout is indicated.

In Act 1 it may be useful to have some chairs and a table permanently in place to represent the Scholls' home. A flight of stairs, or an equivalent way of reaching a higher level, will be necessary in Act 2 Scene 16, when Hans and Sophie scatter leaflets from a height. Two clearly separate pools of light will probably be the most effective way to stage the interrogations scene (Act 2 Scene 17), when Hans and Sophie are questioned at the same time in two separate rooms. The executions at the end (Scene 20) might be staged in a variety of ways – purely symbolically; in silhouette; in black light theatre★, if the facilities are available; and so on.

Otherwise, as long as there's an open space (referred to as the 'open area' in the text) for characters to meet and talk in, there's plenty of room for imagination and experimentation in staging the play. Characters can carry essential props on and off as they enter and exit. Appropriate lighting and costume can also clarify and contribute to the feel of what's happening onstage, but should never hold up the action. If you're prepared to try things out, you'll find the right way for *your* group to put this on in *your* acting space.

Good luck!

Adrian

Lighting and Sound Effects

Lighting can be used to good effect in several scenes – see above. Sounds offstage are needed in:

Act 1 Scene 8   A doorbell
Act 2 Scene 9   A steam train, idling in the station, then
                 getting up steam to move off

★ Black light theatre creates the illusion of normally inanimate objects moving around the stage, through the use of a blacked out stage and actors dressed completely in black moving bright objects.

Costumes and Props

Items you may wish to include:

Hans (Early scenes) Hitler Youth uniform, with dagger in its sheath, and swastika armband. Other Hitler Youths can simply wear the armbands. In later scenes Hans wears a long coat and a German Army uniform, as does his brother, Werner.

Sophie League of German Girls uniform

Other uniforms may be worn for Gestapo Officers (Act 1 Scene 10), a Brownshirt (Act 2 Scene 2), S.S. Guards, with guns (Act 2 Scene 14), Riot Police (Act 2 Scene 14), and Prison Guards (Act 2 Scene 19).

Reichhart Various specific items of dress, at different times: tuxedo jacket, bow-tie (old-fashioned type), top hat, leather gloves

Schmid A broom

Props required in specific scenes:
Scholls' living-room: table and chairs
Hans's lodgings: desk covered with books, and a chair

Act 1

Scenes 3 and 6	Home-made banner with green beast
Scene 6	Swastika banner
Scene 13	Bottle of wine and two teacups

Act 2

Scenes 1, 13, 15, 16	A quantity of leaflets
Scene 1	Hand-cranked duplicating machine
Scene 2	Picnic basket, seven glasses, a bottle of wine and some string
Scene 6	Paint and brushes
Scene 9	Picks, shovels, bar of chocolate and a flower
Scene 11	Shaving mirror and brush
Scene 13	Rucksack
Scene 15	Old-fashioned leather suitcase

Characters

The Scholl Family

Hans	15 years old	
Sophie	13 years old	
Inge	17 years old	(at the start of the play)
Werner	12 years old	
Robert	The children's father; an accountant	
Magdalene	The children's mother; formerly a nurse	

Friends

Luise   A Jewish girl
Ernst   Inge's boyfriend

Hitler Youth

A Youth Leader
Hitler Youths 1, 2, 3 and 4

At the University

Professor Huber
Jakob Schmid   A caretaker
Alex Schmorrel
Traute Lafrenz
Willi Graf   Students
Christoph Probst
Herta Probst   Christoph's wife
Governor Giesler   The Governor of Munich and Bavaria
Student
Other students   (Non-speaking)
Tutors   (Non-speaking)

In the English Park

A Brownshirt   A member of Hitler's militia
A Jewish man   (Non-speaking)

In Poland

A supervisor
A Jewish prisoner
Other prisoners   (Non-speaking)

Police and Prison Service

Johann Reichhart
The Assistant
Gestapo 1
Gestapo 2
Robert Mohr   } Detectives in the Gestapo
Anton Mahler
Prison Guard 1
Prison Guard 2

In Court

Roland Freisler   The judge
Prosecutor
Defence Lawyer
Clerk of the Court
Crowd member

Others

Voice of Radio   A news-reader
Chorus   A team of actors with individual and group speeches
and chants

You will notice that this play features the stage direction 'Beat'. This indicates a split-second hesitation.

ACT 1

SCENE 1

1933/34. The living-room of the Scholls' house.

Robert Scholl *is reading a newspaper.* ***Magdalene Scholl*** *is doing some embroidery.* ***Hans****, wearing his new Hitler Youth uniform, is showing* ***Werner****,* ***Inge*** *and* ***Sophie*** *the dagger he has been presented with on joining.*

The ***Chorus*** *and the* ***Voice of Radio*** *stand at the front of the stage and address the audience.*

Chorus	Attention! Attention! Please stand by.
VoR	30th January 1933. After the chaos of recent days, the President of the Republic has replaced the Chancellor, Franz Von Papen.
Chorus	Attention! Attention! Please stand by.

12

VoR.	A new Chancellor of Germany will head a coalition government.
Chorus	Attention! Attention! Please stand by.
VoR	The leader of Parliament, Hermann Goering, says this signals the start of the National Socialist revolution.
Chorus	*[In a fading chant]* Attention! Attention! Please stand by. Attention! Attention! Please stand by. Attention! Attention! Please stand by.

*The **Chorus** and the **Voice of Radio** go off.*

Hans	What do you think?
Werner	*[Reaching for dagger]* It's fantastic. Can I hold it?
Magdalene	Hans, don't let your brother play with knives.
Hans	*[Keeping hold of dagger]* I won't, mother.
Werner	*[Quietly]* Go on, Hans.
Sophie	What's written on it?
Hans	'Blood and Honour'.
Robert	*[Behind newspaper]* Huh!
Hans	It's not about spilling blood, father. It's about our race. Being part of a great people.
Inge	It's beautiful.
Werner	Will I get one when I join?
Hans	Of course.
Werner	Fantastic! *[he makes a stabbing gesture]*
Hans	*[Putting knife back in sheath]* Mother's right, Werner. It's not a toy. Being a member is a serious business.
Robert	*[Behind newspaper]* Hah!
Magdalene	Robert, it's good for boys to join clubs and have challenges. It gives them pride in themselves.

13

Inge	The uniform's smart.
Sophie	It really suits you, Hans.
Hans	*[Secretly flattered]* Rubbish, Sophie! It's practical, that's all.
Sophie	It's better than the Girls' League. Our skirts are so long, they make hiking impossible.
Hans	I admit our leaders look smart. When you're put in charge of a troop, you wear a green and white braid. And three stars *[taps his shoulder]* ... right here.
Werner	I bet you get your own troop before long.
Hans	I mean to try.
Robert	*[Behind newspaper]* Pah!
Inge	If we admire you any more Hans, you'll get big-headed. Anyway, it's time I went out.
Magdalene	Going anywhere nice, Inge?
Inge	Seeing some friends in the park, that's all.
Sophie	Is Ernst going to be there?

14

Inge	Maybe.
Sophie	Say 'hello' from me, won't you?
Werner	[*To **Hans***] Sophie's mad about Ernst as well.
Sophie	[*Embarrassed*] That's not true. You know it isn't.
Magdalene	Tell Ernst he's welcome to tea, any day.
Robert	[*Behind newspaper*] Huh!
Inge	Perhaps.
Robert	[*Puts down paper and takes some coins from his pocket*] Since you must have a boyfriend, ask Ernst to pop into a tobacconist for me.
Inge	[*Embarrassed*] He's not my boyfriend!
Robert	I've run out of cigars. You know the ones I like. Best get them from Springers.
Inge	[*Taking coins*] Oh . . .
Hans	Springers? No one goes there now.
Werner	It's boycotted.
Robert	Manni Springer knows how to look after cigars. He doesn't let them dry out. [*to **Inge***] Please. From Springers.
Inge	All right father. [*going off*] I won't be back late.
Magdalene	Enjoy yourself, Inge.
Werner	[*Mimicking **Inge***] 'Oh, Ernst, how lovely to see you. You look so handsome.'
Sophie	[*Swipes her brother*] Shut up, Werner!
Robert	[*To **Hans***] I'm surprised they don't give you a sheep's head as well.
Hans	Pardon?
Robert	As part of your outfit.

Hans	That's a foolish thing to say, father.
Magdalene	Hans!
Robert	That's how they want you to behave, isn't it? Like sheep?
Hans	Yes, well. We all know how you feel about wearing uniforms –
Magdalene	*[Over]* Don't talk to your father like that!
Robert	Let the boy speak his mind. If you've something to say, you can say it. That's the rule in this house.
Hans	*[Points to his uniform]* I'm proud of this.
Robert	And proud of the man it represents?
Hans	Look around you. People are working again. The bread queues are disappearing.
Robert	But what kind of work? Building weapons and work-camps!
Sophie	That's not fair! You know my friend Luise at school? Her father's just got a job.
Magdalene	That's true, Robert. The first decent one he's had in years.
Sophie	He's surveying the new road to Munich.
Werner	I'd like that. Working outdoors all day.
Hans	You see, father? What's wrong with road-building?
Robert	But what's going to be travelling on the new roads?
Hans	*[Sarcastically]* Traffic, maybe.
	Sophie *and* ***Werner*** *laugh.*
Robert	Soldiers, more likely. I kept my eyes on the National Socialists, when no one thought they mattered. Thugs in brown shirts, that's what people said. But I knew there was more to that jumped up little Austrian corporal –
Hans	*[Angrily]* At least he fought in the war! He didn't refuse combat duty like you did.
Magdalene	Hans! That's quite enough.

16

Sophie	*[To **Robert**]* You always think the worst of the Chancellor.
Robert	I'm not denying he's clever, Sophie. He knows how to play on our fears. Of unemployment. Of other people. That's why we voted him and his cronies a little bit of power. Only to see him snatch all the rest, by getting rid of parliament.
Hans	You're so unfair to him!
Werner	Hear! hear!
Sophie	You don't understand, father. The National Socialists only want to make Germany great again.
Robert	They want us to be sheep, because they are wolves.
Hans	*[Furious]* I give up! You're completely stuck in the past.
Magdalene	Calm down.
Hans	*[Moving off]* And I won't listen to any more cynical rubbish about Hitler. *[turns to **Werner** and **Sophie**]* Coming?
	Werner and Sophie follow Hans off.
Magdalene	Was that really necessary, Robert?
	Robert shrugs and raises the newspaper again.
	*Lights down on the living-room. **Robert** and **Magdalene** go off.*

• •

SCENE 2

22 February 1943. The open area.

Reichhart and Assistant come on. The Assistant tries to polish Reichhart's shoes throughout the scene, although Reichhart won't keep still.

Reichhart	That's what I don't understand. They were such good children.
Assistant	Hans especially.
Reichhart	His sister, Sophie, too. When they were young, they welcomed the National Socialists coming to power. They saw fresh, pure

17

blood in Germany's veins and, like all right-thinking people, they were glad.

Assistant	So where did they go wrong?
Reichhart	That's the troubling question. *[points to shoe]* The toe's filthy!
Assistant	Sorry, Johann.
Reichhart	Leave one speck of dirt, and there'll be trouble.
Assistant	I won't. I promise.
Reichhart	We may very well be needed this afternoon.
Assistant	I know, I know.
Reichhart	They say Himmler* himself is taking an interest.
Assistant	I promise you'll look your best.
Reichhart	I'd better. If we're called on to act, we must look the part.
Assistant	Of course.
Reichhart	Appearance is everything. Flags, lights, uniforms. That's how it works. A uniform makes you feel part of something bigger, more important than yourself. Is there any better feeling?
Assistant	No, Johann. Absolutely not.
Reichhart	Hans Scholl understood that at first. *[starts to move off]* Show me the jacket.
Assistant	Right away.
Reichhart	*[Stops at the edge of the stage]* No young man tried harder in the Hitler Youth. That's the great tragedy. *[goes off stage; calls]* It had better be spotless.
Assistant	*[Hurrying off]* It is, Johann. Very nearly.

* Heinrich Himmler was one of the most powerful men in Nazi Germany and controlled the Gestapo.

SCENE 3

1936. A hall.

*Hans comes on in front of a group of **Hitler Youths** in uniform. They are carrying a large flag between them, which has the outline of a great mythical beast partly sewn on.*

Hans	OK. Lay it down carefully.
Hitler Youth 1	Do we have to do this, Hans?
Hitler Youth 2	Sewing is girls' work.
Hans	If a comrade gashes his leg when we're mountain-climbing and you sew up the wound to save his life – is that girls' work?
Hitler Youth 2	I guess not.
Hans	Of course it isn't. And neither's this. The great beast we're putting on the flag –
Hitler Youth 3	*[Over]* It looks like a dragon.
Hitler Youth 1	*[Over]* More like a gryphon. Those are lion's claws.
Hans	– is our very own mascot. Strong and fierce, like our troop.
Hitler Youth 4	*[Indicating **Hitler Youth 2**]* Klaus eats too many plum tarts to be strong and fierce.
Hitler Youth 2	No I don't!
Hans	When we take this to rallies, it'll show we're the most imaginative group in Bavaria. We'll tell tales about the fierce Prussian monsters it's slain.
Hitler Youth 2	Yes!

*The **Youth Leader** comes in. The boys stand to attention.*

Youth Leader	Relax boys. I've some good news. *[the boys stand at ease]* Hans?
Hans	Sir?
Youth Leader	Your enthusiasm and diligence have been noted. I spoke with some of my superiors and we have a little present for you.

Hans	*[Puzzled]* Thank you, sir.
Youth Leader	*[Taking something from his pocket]* Nothing much. Only a piece of braid and three small stars. *[he holds them out to **Hans**]*
Hans	*[Hardly believing his luck]* Do you mean . . .?
Youth Leader	*[Teasing]* Don't you want to be a troop leader?
Hans	Very much so, sir. *[takes the braid and the stars]* Thank you.
Youth Leader	*[To the other **Hitler Youth**]* Is he a good choice?
Hitler Youth 3	Definitely.
Hitler Youth 1	Hans is the best.
Youth Leader	Now continue with your task, boys.
Hans	Yes, sir.
Hitler Youth 2	Can we have some music while we're working? Can Hans fetch his guitar, sir?
Youth Leader	Why not?
Hans	Thanks.
Youth Leader	Just one thing.
Hans	Sir?
Youth Leader	Not the foreign songs you play sometimes. Nothing Norwegian or Russian.
Hans	*[Surprised]* Oh. Right, sir.
Youth Leader	We can't have the world thinking there are no good German tunes, can we?

Youth Leader, Hans and the rest of the Hitler Youth go off with the flag.

1936. A street.

Sophie, in her League of German Girls uniform, comes on with her friend Luise, who is wearing ordinary clothes.

Luise	Well, go on. Show me.
Sophie	It looks stupid, Luise.
Luise	Go on.
Sophie	*[Looks round to see no one else is watching]* All right. Like this. *[she marches across the stage, swinging her arms]* Right turn! *[she turns round, marches back and stops]*
Luise	*[Trying not to laugh]* That's tremendous, Sophie!
Sophie	*[Laughing]* We do it for hours. I know I look ridiculous.
Luise	No you don't.
Sophie	Luise.
Luise	Well, maybe just a little. But it's worth it to be a member.
Sophie	We're going camping by the lake on Saturday. Forty of us.
Luise	That'll be fun.
Sophie	I know. I love sitting round campfires in the dark. Sometimes, when I lean back to look up at the stars, I start laughing. I can't help it. It's the most wonderful feeling. To be part of something so extraordinary as this world.
Luise	You're making me envious.
Sophie	And then there's always singing. Telling stories ... *[with relish]* Gossiping.
Luise	You'll have to tell me all the news when you get back.
Sophie	I will. And what about you? Is Albert still waiting on the corner every time your mother sends you shopping?
Luise	*[Seriously]* No.

Sophie	You haven't argued with him?
Luise	He stopped talking to me. As soon as he found out.
Sophie	*[Sadly]* Oh.
Luise	Everyone on the street's heard father lost his job on the new road. *[quoting]* 'Not suitable'.
Sophie	I'm sorry, Luise.
Luise	It's all right. We're getting used to people looking the other way when they see us. Not stopping to chat.
Sophie	That's dreadful.
Luise	One or two still smile when no one's looking. And I don't want Albert for a boyfriend, anyway. He's so boring.
Sophie	*[Pulling a face]* And ugly.
Luise	Yes! *[beat]* But I still wish I could join the Girls' League and come camping with you.

Sophie and *Luise* go off.

● ●

SCENE 5

1936. The living-room in the Scholls' house.

Robert, Magdalene, Hans, Werner and *Inge* are finishing a light meal at the table.

Magdalene	*[To Inge]* So you're going out with Ernst again?
Inge	*[Trying to sound casual]* He's got no one else to go with. And since I don't mind dancing –
Werner	*[Over]* You've been seeing him for ages now. Are you going to marry him, Inge?
Inge	Don't be ridiculous!
Robert	Werner, stop being impertinent.
Magdalene	And don't speak when your mouth's full.

Hans	Well, if Inge hasn't got any more news about Ernst, I've something quite interesting to tell you.
Magdalene	What's that, dear?
Hans	I'm going to be a flag bearer for the whole town.
Robert	You're always carrying that damn flag.
Hans	Not just here in Ulm. *[proudly]* At this year's Party Day Rally.
Inge	You're going to Nuremberg?
Hans	In September. I know it's still months away, but it'll be the biggest one yet.
Werner	You'll see the Führer*. You lucky devil!
Robert	Language!
Magdalene	You will be careful, won't you?
Hans	There's nothing to worry about, mother. It'll be wonderful.
Robert	So the Pied Piper's got his flute out again and you can't wait to run after him?
Magdalene	Robert, you can understand why Hans is excited.
Hans	It's a great honour, father.
	Sophie comes on.
Inge	*[To Hans]* Congratulations.
Sophie	Sorry I'm late. *[she joins the others]*
Magdalene	It's all right, dear.
Inge	Werner wanted to eat the last piece of cake, but I've saved it for you.
Sophie	Thanks.
Hans	The Company Leader said I was the obvious choice to go.
Werner	You're going to be jealous, Sophie.

* Führer – meaning 'leader' in German, it is often used for Adolf Hitler.

Magdalene	*[Disapproving]* Werner!
Sophie	Why?
Werner	Ernst's taking Inge to a dance tonight. On their own.
Magdalene	Don't be silly.
Werner	Everyone knows Sophie's got a crush on Ernst.
Sophie	No I haven't.
Inge	A little bird tells me she's becoming very close to someone called Fritz.
Sophie	Inge!
Magdalene	Fritz? Fritz Hartnagel?
Sophie	We're friends, that's all.
Inge	She's very mopey when he's not around.
Magdalene	Oh, I like Fritz. He's such a well-mannered boy.
Hans	*[Tired of being ignored]* And I won't simply *see* the Führer. I'll hear him speak as well.
Robert	How unfortunate for you.
Sophie	What's happening?
Werner	Hans is going to the Party Day Rally in September.
Hans	*[With false modesty]* I suppose I was just lucky to be chosen.
Sophie	*[Unenthusiastically]* Well done.
Hans	Thank you. Though I guessed they'd ask me. The Company Leader's always praising my attitude –
Magdalene	*[Cutting in]* That's enough now, Hans. *[to **Sophie**]* How was Luise?
Sophie	Her father's lost his job.
Inge	No!
Magdalene	The poor man.

Sophie	And they still won't let her join the Girls' League. It's crazy. She's got bright blue eyes. She looks more Aryan than I do.
Robert	Why expect fairness from the bunch of gangsters we've got in power?
Magdalene	*[Long-suffering]* Robert.
Hans	They're not gangsters!
Robert	No?
Inge	*[Trying to change the subject]* There's a new band playing at the dance. They're meant to be very good.
Magdalene	Really?
Robert	If they're not gangsters, then what happened to Rolf Schulze?
Werner	Who?
Magdalene	Oh yes. That *was* terrible.
Hans	Rolf Schulze?
Inge	My old maths teacher.
Robert	Simply because he refused to join the correct union last month, a whole squad of Brownshirts walked past him, spitting in his face.
Sophie	Oh no!
Hans	Well, of course that's awful.
Robert	And now Rolf's disappeared.
Magdalene	Disappeared?
Robert	I heard it from his father. No one knows where he is. His parents can't get any sense from the authorities.
Hans	I'm not defending what some of the Brownshirts do.
Robert	I should hope not. We've brought you up better than that.
Hans	But you mustn't judge the whole movement from a few stupid individuals.
Robert	A few? They're everywhere.

Hans	Say what you like father, but you have to admit the streets are a lot safer now. There's much less crime.
Werner	Hans is right.
Robert	Only because the criminals are in power themselves. And what about crimes against the human spirit?
Magdalene	Can't we have one meal where we don't argue?
Inge	I agree.
Robert	We're not allowed to think for ourselves any more.
Hans	Rubbish!
Robert	Then why does everyone look over their shoulder before expressing an opinion these days?
Sophie	That's true, Hans.
Werner	If Hitler was so bad, no one would have come to the Olympic Games this summer.
Hans	Well said, Werner.
Werner	Now the whole world's buzzing about us. Journalists came from England, America. All over. They like the New Germany.
Hans	And that's entirely thanks to the Führer. He's a great man.
Robert	*[Exasperated]* Haven't I taught you children anything!
Magdalene	*[Calming]* Robert.
Robert	Never mind what anyone else says or does. The most important thing is to be true to yourself and to God. Don't worship false idols.
Sophie	Nobody's worshipping Hitler.
Robert	That's what Doctor Goebbels* wants us to do with his beloved Adolf, isn't it? You can't buy a pair of underpants without that madman's eyes staring down at you from the wall of the shop.

* Goebbels was Hitler's propoganda minister, taking control of the news media and ensuring the Nazi way of thinking was put across.

Werner	*[Sniggers]* Underpants!
Magdalene	*[To Robert]* There's no need to be vulgar.
Hans	Hitler's not a madman. He's a visionary.
Robert	If he's so honourable and good, why doesn't he allow people to talk freely about his wonderful government? Instead of closing down newspapers and putting snoopers into every block of flats.
Hans	That's a malicious rumour.
Robert	One that I happen to believe. *[standing up; sarcastic]* Now I'm going to risk a prison sentence by listening to the news. On Swiss Radio.
Hans	What's wrong with the German stations?
Robert	Everything. Come and help me tune in, Werner. You're good at that kind of thing.
Werner	*[Getting up]* OK. *[he follows Robert off stage]*
Magdalene	*[Getting up.]* Will you help with the dishes, Inge?
Inge	*[Getting up]* I want to get ready.
Magdalene	You've still got plenty of time.
	Magdalene takes some plates off stage, followed by Inge, who does the same.
Sophie	Why's dad in such a foul mood?
Hans	He doesn't want me going to Nuremberg, I suppose.
Sophie	You've done well to be chosen.
Hans	You don't sound very excited.
Sophie	I was a little upset when I came in.
Hans	Why?
Sophie	Luise.
Hans	Oh yes. It's unfortunate about her father.

Sophie	Why does it matter so much, Hans? So what, if her family's Jewish?
Hans	The way I understand it, the party isn't against Jews as such. In fact, the Führer is said to be the most tolerant of men. It's more a question of loyalty to your own race. After the war –
Sophie	*[Over]* Lots of Jews fought for us then.
Hans	I know.
Sophie	Annie Weinberg's grandfather died at the Somme.
Hans	*[Awkwardly]* Look, Sophie. When Hitler became Chancellor, Germany was on its knees. We'd been bled dry by the Treaty of Versailles –
Sophie	*[Over]* I understand that. I do listen in school.
Hans	We were a laughing-stock. Well, Hitler's put an end to all that, hasn't he? No one laughed when our soldiers took back the Rhineland.
Sophie	No. I suppose not.
Hans	He's shown we can't be bullied any more. That's why he's brought back conscription.
Sophie	Is he getting ready for another war?
Hans	No! That's simply foreign propaganda. The Führer has promised we won't take any more land. But we need a proper army, so that France and England won't pick on us. We're becoming strong again. We can be proud of our country. And that's all because of Hitler.
Sophie	It just seems unfair that Luise can't come camping with us.
Hans	I agree, what's happening with the Jews isn't quite right. I'm sorry for Luise. She's a nice girl. But things get mixed up when a country's changing so fast. They'll get sorted, soon enough. We simply have to put our faith in the party and our leader. You'll see.

Sophie, unconvinced, smiles and shrugs. She and Hans go off.

1936. A hall.

*The **Youth Leader** comes on.*

Youth Leader   *[Looking off]* Come on boys. We must drill until we're perfect.

*The troop of **Hitler Youths**, except **Hitler Youths 2** and **4**, marches on. When they are all onstage, they march on the spot. **Hans** comes on carrying a large swastika flag and goes to the front.*

That's it! Keep in step! Take your lead from Hans. Remember, the eyes of the world will be on you in Nuremberg. There'll be radio and film crews everywhere. You'll be movie stars, boys.

***Hitler Youth 2** and **Hitler Youth 4** hurry on, carrying the mythical beast flag between them. They try to join the others.*

Stop! *[all the boys stop marching; to **Hitler Youth 2**]* What do you think you're doing, Klaus?

Hitler Youth 2	We forgot this, sir. Our own flag.
Youth Leader	I thought you knew. It's no longer permitted to use irregular banners. Throw it away.
Hitler Youth 4	But it took hours to make.
Youth Leader	*[Annoyed]* Pardon?
Hitler Youth 2	We worked very hard on it sir.
Youth Leader	Don't you understand what I said?
Hitler Youth 4	It's a special design for Ulm, sir.
Youth Leader	Throw it away!

Hitler Youth 2 and Hitler Youth 4 exchange glances. Hitler Youth 4 lets go of his side of the flag, but Hitler Youth 2 keeps hold.

Throw it away, boy!

Hitler Youth 2 starts to tremble with fear, but keeps hold of the flag. The Youth Leader pulls his hand back to hit him. Hans steps forward to stop him.

Scholl! What do you think you're doing?

Hans	*[Quietly and calmly]* Don't hit him.
Youth Leader	What?
Hans	We all helped make the flag. It means a lot to our troop, sir.
Youth Leader	It's not for us to decide what has meaning! Why have a leadership if everyone is to think for themselves? That's communistic thinking. It has no place in a National Socialist state. Do you understand, boy?

Hans and the Youth Leader stare aggressively at each other for a moment, before they both turn away. They, and all the Hitler Youth, go off.

SCENE 7

22 February 1943 and September 1936. The open area.

Reichhart comes on wearing a tuxedo jacket. The Assistant follows, brushing the tuxedo with a clothes brush from time to time.

Reichhart	What a mood to get himself into before Nuremberg.
Assistant	His parents are to blame if you ask me. Didn't bring him up properly.
Reichhart	Going to the rally should have straightened him out. I always found them inspirational.
Assistant	I went to one, you know.
Reichhart	I went to many. Wonderful occasions. A chance to see the whole leadership and hear its vision of the future.

While Reichhart and the Assistant continue speaking, large swastikas unfurl at the back of the stage as the Chorus comes on. They spread out and face upstage, stepping silently in military rhythm.

Assistant	I remember thousands and thousands of party members filling Adolf Hitler Platz. Marching. Drilling –
Reichhart	Everywhere you looked, there were flags. A whole ocean of swastikas. Simply magnificent!
Assistant	Even better, when night fell.
Reichhart	Brilliant white searchlights reaching up to the sky!
Assistant	Fireworks exploding everywhere!
Reichhart	Brightest of all was the Führer. The one who had finally brought light out of Germany's darkness.

Hans comes on, and walks, with growing distaste, through the crowd.

Assistant	And didn't the music stir your blood? The 'Horst Wessel' song? The 'Badenweiler'?

ACT 1 SCENE 7

31

Reichhart	I loved the marches. When you felt the rhythm pulsing in your body, you started to melt. The whole square joined together as one. We were a single Germany. Under a single leader.
Assistant	Did you ever hear him speak?
Reichhart	Oh yes! What an experience. Hundreds of thousands of us waiting. Every pair of eyes straining to see him appear on the podium. Oh, and the thunderous roar of 'Heil Hitler!' when he did. My eyes filled with tears. I was in heaven.
Assistant	And such wisdom in his words.
Reichhart	After the anarchy we'd been through, the country was crying out for leadership.

*The members of the **Chorus** turn to face the audience as they deliver their lines. The sound of their marching feet builds gradually under:*

Chorus 1	Jews no longer have a right to citizenship.
Chorus 2	Marriage between Jews and Aryans is forbidden.
Chorus 3	No Jew may be employed in public office, teaching, farming . . .
Chorus 4	. . . journalism, radio, cinema or theatre.
Chorus 5	There are to be no Jewish lawyers and doctors.
Chorus 6	Our nation has a historic destiny.
Chorus 7	It has a right to reverse the injustices of the past.
Chorus 8	The German-speaking peoples must once more be reunited.
Chorus 9	Given room to thrive.
Chorus 10	The individual must disappear . . .
Chorus 11	. . . to become part of the state, whose decisions are to be made by one man alone.
Chorus 12	And I am that man!

The stamping of feet builds to a tremendous crescendo.

Chorus	Heil Hitler!
Hans	*[Covering his ears]* No!
	*The marching stops. The **Chorus** and **Hans** go silently off.*
Reichhart	It was like a long, cool glass of beer to a man dying of thirst.
Assistant	Magnificent!
Reichhart	I simply don't understand why the boy wasn't inspired.
Assistant	He must have had a heart of stone.
Reichhart	*[Checking his jacket]* What do my shoulders look like?
Assistant	It's a good fit.
Reichhart	The elbows aren't too shiny?
Assistant	Not at all.
Reichhart	It should have been replaced a year ago. But they tell me every scrap of material's needed on the eastern front.
Assistant	They don't appreciate how vital your job is.
Reichhart	No one ever does. *[going off]* Now we must find my tie.
Assistant	*[To himself]* It's completely inexplicable. Why didn't Nuremberg make the boy see sense?

• •

SCENE 8

September 1936. The living-room in the Scholls' house.

*Werner and Sophie are welcoming **Hans** back from the Nuremberg Rally. **Hans** is now wearing a long coat over his Hitler Youth uniform.*

Sophie	So how was it?
Hans	All right.
Werner	Did you see Hitler?

Hans	I saw all of them. Goebbels too. And Doctor Schacht, drinking a coffee.
Werner	What's he like? The Führer?
Hans	A man. The same as any other.
Sophie	Didn't you enjoy yourself?
Hans	*[Guarded]* It was all right, Sophie.
Werner	I wish I'd gone instead. I'd've had a great time.
Sophie	*[Wants a moment alone with **Hans**]* Werner. Get the papers that came for Hans.
Werner	Oh yes! You've been waiting for these. *[he goes off]*
Sophie	You didn't enjoy it? *[**Hans** shrugs]* What was wrong with the rally?
Hans	Nothing. *[beat; more honestly]* Father was right. It was a little like a sheep-market. The idiots on the campsite kept joking about . . . *[trails off]*
Sophie	About what?
Hans	How many heads they'd cracked open. Gypsies and communists. Boys who they considered effeminate.
Sophie	They boasted about bullying?
Hans	All the time. They expected me to laugh, but I didn't.
Sophie	Of course not.
	The doorbell rings.
Hans	Everyone spoke about loyalty. Being loyal to our country. Being loyal to the Führer. Doing what he says without question. But I kept remembering father's motto. What about being true to yourself?
Sophie	*[Quoting her father]* 'And to God –'
Hans	*[Quoting his father]* '– no matter what anyone else says'.

Werner comes on with Ernst.

Werner	He can't keep away, can he?
Hans	Hello, Ernst.
Ernst	Hello. Hi, Sophie.
Sophie	Hi.
Ernst	Is Inge around? I'm meant to be taking her to the cinema.
Sophie	She's upstairs, getting ready. *[going off]* I'll tell her you're here.
Ernst	Thanks.
Werner	*[Handing Hans a letter]* This is what came for you.
Hans	*[Takes letter]* It must be my call-up date. *[opens letter and reads]*
Ernst	I'm starting my army service as well.
Werner	*[Sarcastic]* Poor Inge. It'll break her heart.
Hans	Werner, go and do your homework.
Werner	But it's so boring.
Hans	Hurry up and go.
Werner	All right. Tch! *[walks off slowly]*
Hans	I'm sorry about my little brother.
Ernst	Don't worry. Where are you doing your service?
Hans	I'm lucky. They're letting me join a cavalry regiment.
Ernst	Inge says you're quite a horseman.
Hans	So-so.
Ernst	Two years in the army means we'll be old men by the time we go to university. Do you still want to study medicine?
Hans	That's the idea.

Ernst	It's a good choice. If our government carries on being so aggressive, we'll soon need a lot of doctors. *[worried that he's said too much]* Sorry! That sounds disloyal to the Führer.
Hans	It's all right, Ernst.
Ernst	I didn't mean to criticise him.
Hans	It's OK. I'm starting to think a little differently about him myself.
Ernst	*[Cautiously]* Really?
Hans	I've decided to leave the Hitler Youth. I'm tired of being told what to think.
Ernst	Well – if you're still interested in doing some walking and climbing before you join the army –
Hans	*[Over]* Very much so.
Ernst	There is another organization you can join. 'Young Germans'.
Hans	I thought that was banned.
Ernst	It is. It's not Nazi, so of course it's banned. *[quietly amused]* But we still meet up secretly and organize trips. It's not political. It's just for fun. We talk about whatever we want to. Play music sometimes.
Hans	Only German music?
Ernst	No. Whatever we like. No one worries where it comes from, as long as it's good. We're a bunch of free spirits.
Hans	Then I'm definitely interested in joining.

Hans and Ernst go off.

SCENE 9

22 February 1943. The open area.

Reichhart comes on, followed by the Assistant, who is now wearing a bow-tie.

Reichhart   Investigators say you could smell subversion in the Scholls' house.

Assistant   Would you believe it? They listened to foreign radio stations!

Reichhart   I'm not surprised.

Assistant   Can you imagine the filth Hans and Sophie must have heard?

Reichhart   Only too easily. Lies about German rearmament. Pure fiction about the treatment of undesirables in the Reich.

Assistant   No wonder the Propaganda Minister banned radios which received foreign broadcasts.

Reichhart   German stations only! We must be restricted to hearing the truth.

Assistant   *[Disgusted]* Hans Scholl's mind was completely corrupted. Imagine joining 'Young Germans'! A forbidden organization!

Reichhart   Admittedly only for climbing and hiking. But once you break one rule, where does it stop?

Assistant   With us, Johann.

Reichhart   Always with us. *[notices the Assistant's tie]* You must get yourself another tie.

Assistant   But this one's new.

Reichhart   That's why I'm taking it. *[removes the Assistant's bow-tie]*

Assistant   But where will I find – *[Reichhart cuts him off with a look]* Very well. *[he goes off]*

Reichhart   *[Looking round; to himself]* Hans and Sophie can't complain about injustice. They could have stopped at any time. They were given a very clear warning. *[he goes off]*

ACT 1   SCENE 9

37

SCENE 10

1938. The living-room of the Scholls' house.

Robert and **Magdalene** *come on at one side.* **Sophie** *and* **Gestapo Officer 1** *come on at the other.*

Magdalene	Are you all right, Sophie?
Gestapo 1	She's fine.
Robert	Have they treated you properly?
Sophie	I've no complaints.
Gestapo 1	It was a purely routine arrest and investigation.
Sophie	All they did was put me in a cell and ask a few questions.
Gestapo 1	There's no charge to answer, so I've brought her home.
Magdalene	What about our other children?
Gestapo 1	They'll be dealt with in due course.
Robert	You haven't heard the last of this!
Magdalene	*[Quietly warning]* Robert –
Robert	I'll complain to your bosses.
Gestapo 1	You're welcome to, Mr Scholl. See how far you get. *[starting to go]* Now, excuse me.
Robert	Gladly.
Gestapo 1	But you should keep a closer eye on your children. Before they get into serious trouble. *[he goes off]*
Magdalene	*[Hugs Sophie]* Have they hurt you?
Sophie	No, I'm fine. It's the others we need to worry about.
Robert	I've contacted Hans's regiment. His captain says he'll speak up for him. As for Inge and Werner – the police'll huff and puff a little, then let them go like everyone else, I expect.
Magdalene	But why were you all arrested?

Sophie	They kept asking me about 'Young Germans'. How long was Hans a member? Does he read forbidden literature?
Magdalene	I knew it was dangerous for him to join.
Sophie	I didn't tell them anything.
Robert	[To *Magdalene*] It's a good job you cleared the boys' room when the police came.
Sophie	What happened?
Robert	Your mother was very brave.
Magdalene	Nonsense! I was a nurse wasn't I? I'm used to emergencies.
Sophie	What did you do?
Magdalene	While the officers were searching in here, I swept all the boys' magazines into a basket, covered it with a cloth and asked, very sweetly, if I could run to the bakers.
Robert	As soon as she was outside, she got rid of the magazines.
Sophie	Well done! If the Gestapo knew Hans and Werner were reading anti-Nazi literature, there'd be real trouble.
Magdalene	But 'Young Germans' is nothing more than a walking group. Why should the Nazis arrest its members and their families?
Robert	Because they're afraid of their own shadows these days. They want to take over Austria. Czechoslovakia too. So they think everyone else is as crooked as they are.
Magdalene	[To *Sophie*] I spoke to Mrs Reden. Ernst has been arrested as well.
Sophie	Inge will be so upset.
Robert	That boy doesn't have a political bone in his body.
Magdalene	There's a kind of madness taking over the country.
Robert	We've known that for years.

Magdalene	But now it's getting worse. You can't trust anyone. When they came to power, I thought: 'Not to worry. The Nazis are so busy fighting amongst themselves, they won't last long.' But I was wrong. Every day, their grip gets tighter.

● ●

SCENE 11

1938. The open area.

*The **Voice of Radio** comes on with the **Chorus**. Each member of the **Chorus** carries a small box, which rattles when shaken.*

Chorus	Attention! Attention! Please stand by.
VoR	November 1938. Criminal protests against Germany's racial and territorial policies continue. It is with great regret we announce a secretary in our French Embassy has been assassinated.
Chorus	Attention! Attention! Please stand by.
VoR	Murdered by a German Jewish refugee. Naturally all right-minded people will wish to respond. Police have been instructed not to interfere with any spontaneous demonstrations of outrage.
Chorus	Attention! Attention! Please stand by.
VoR	The Security Service warns that synagogues are only to be burnt down if there is no danger of fire spreading to German businesses. Jewish homes and workplaces may be destroyed, but not looted. After all, we are not criminals.

*The **Chorus** begins to rattle the boxes increasingly loudly under:*

Chorus	*[Chanting]* Windows, synagogues, businesses, homes. Windows, synagogues, businesses, homes. *[they repeat the chant with increasing volume and ferocity until finally shouting together]* Shatter! Shatter! Shatter!

*The **Chorus** goes off, murmuring the 'Windows, synagogues, businesses, homes' refrain. The **Voice of Radio** goes off.*

22 February 1943. The open area.

Reichhart *comes on, putting on his bow-tie. The* ***Assistant*** *follows.*

Reichhart	So much chaos everywhere, on 'The Night of Broken Glass'. Synagogues destroyed. Shops burnt down.
Assistant	And the mobs! Violent deaths everywhere.
Reichhart	It shook a few people up, didn't it? Hans and Sophie Scholl should have taken the hint. The National Socialists were serious about changing Germany . . . Is my tie presentable?
Assistant	It's hanging a little to the right.
Reichhart	*[Adjusting tie]* But they simply wouldn't listen. When Hans was released from the army to study medicine here in Munich, he fell in with the wrong crowd straight away.
Assistant	*[Looking at tie]* Now it's hanging a little to the left.

Hans *comes on from one side of the stage;* ***Christoph Probst*** *and* ***Alex Schmorell*** *from the other.*

Reichhart	Somehow subversives always sniff each other out. I don't know how. Maybe it's the way they talk. Certain words they use. Perhaps it's just their smell . . . However it happens, Hans soon made friends with other like-minded medical students.

Hans, Christoph and Alex meet and talk in mime.

Assistant	Oh, I know. There was a whole gang, wasn't there?
Reichhart	Christoph Probst and Alex Schmorell were the first. Both of them had completely the wrong attitude to National Socialism. Fortunately, Christoph was too busy with his young family to be much of a nuisance. But Alex was a very bad sort. His mother was Russian, so what can you expect? Soon he was walking with Hans along the slippery path of treason.
Assistant	Now your tie is hanging down on both sides.
Reichhart	*[Takes tie off in exasperation]* Then come and do it for me! *[goes off]*
Assistant	*[Going off]* Willingly, Johann.

Christoph waves goodbye to Alex and Hans, then goes off. Alex and Hans move to:

• •

SCENE 13

1 September 1939. Hans's student lodgings in Munich.

Hans pours from a bottle of wine into two tea cups and gives one to Alex.

Hans	How do you know I'll like her, Alex?
Alex	I just know.
Hans	She might be a boring little Nazi and disapprove of every book on my shelves.
Alex	OK. Two reasons I know you'll like Traute.
Hans	Go on.

Alex	Firstly, because she's very attractive and you like looking at pretty women.
Hans	Hey! I have a girlfriend at home now. I write to my dear Rose as often as I can.
Alex	You still like ogling any woman with a nice figure.
Hans	Only out of professional interest. I'm training to be a doctor.
Alex	Secondly, Traute's studying medicine. So you have that in common. And thirdly –
Hans	*[Over]* You said 'two reasons' why I'll like her.
Alex	– and thirdly she knows you're a jailbird.
Hans	That 'Young Germans' business? I was only in custody for six weeks before my captain got me out. Hardly a jailbird.
Alex	It's a badge of honour to be arrested by these morons.
Hans	And this girl, Traute? She's not bothered that I've been in trouble with the Gestapo?
Alex	Not at all. She's no more respect for the Nazis than we have.
Hans	Then she's very welcome to join our social circle.
Alex	Christoph's coming with her.
Hans	Does she drink wine or beer?
Alex	I don't know. Wine, I think.
Hans	Good. Because we haven't got any beer.
Alex	*[Looks at wine bottle]* We haven't got much wine left either. *[beat]* Maybe Christoph and Traute won't be thirsty. *[pours the last of the wine into his and **Hans's** tea cups]*
Hans	How terrible it is to be a poor student.
Alex	It's better than the army. I hated national service.
Hans	I enjoyed working with horses. All the rest – 'Yes sir', 'No sir' – made me sick.

Alex	I'm worried they'll call us back soon.
Hans	Any day, the way our ridiculous Führer is behaving.
Alex	What's all this fuss about Poland for?
Hans	It's nonsense. No one's threatening any Germans there.
Alex	It doesn't matter if it's true or not. Hitler's just looking for an excuse to invade.
Hans	That's what it looks like.
Alex	And I don't think the British and French will stand by this time. Hans, what if Hitler drags Germany into a war? And we're called up again?
Hans	It's not a nice thought.
Alex	What's the right thing to do, when you've got lunatics running the government?
Hans	I don't know. I've thought about it a lot. And prayed.
Alex	Sometimes I want to stick my head out of the window and shout 'Wake up everybody! Come to your senses. We're being ruled by madmen.'
Hans	You'd be arrested in minutes and executed in days.
Alex	How's it happened? Professors and engineers scrubbing pavements because of their race. Our troops marching into other countries on a whim.
Hans	Perhaps it's not just us. Perhaps a lot of people feel as angry as we do.
Alex	I don't think so. Look at the crowds who cheer every new crime the Führer commits.
Hans	There are plenty who don't. They're just too afraid to speak out.
Alex	What use is silence? It allows our masters to get away with murder.

Hans	I know.
Alex	And what if we're recalled to service? Are we to be part of the thuggery?
Hans	At least we'll only serve with a medical unit. We'll be trying to save lives, not take them.
Alex	That's the one thing that makes it bearable. All the same –
Hans	*[Over]* It sticks in your throat, doing anything for this lot. But to turn against your own country is a terrible thing.
Alex	I'm not against Germany. It's National Socialism I can't stomach.
Hans	You know the sister I was telling you about?
Alex	Sophie?
Hans	Yes. *[takes a letter from his pocket]* She wrote to me today. She's even angrier than we are.
Alex	What does she say?
Hans	A friend of hers – a Jewish friend – her family's house was burnt down during the anti-Semitic★ demonstrations.
Alex	Two of our neighbours have disappeared since 'The Night of Broken Glass'.
Hans	Sophie doesn't understand how we can produce geniuses like Beethoven and Schiller, yet act like such savages now. *[looks at letter]* She says: 'People like us need a tough spirit, but a tender heart to survive these terrible times.'
Alex	She sounds quite a sister.
Hans	She is. She's hoping to study here when she's finished school and her labour service.
	There's a knock at the door.
Alex	That'll be Christoph and Traute.

★ anti-Semitic – theory or action directed against the Jews

Hans	*[Getting up and brushing his fingers through his hair]* How do I look?
Alex	As hideous as ever. Stop being vain and answer the door.
	Hans goes off to open the door to his apartment. Alex gulps down the last of the wine and hides the empty bottle.
Hans	*[Offstage]* Hi, Christoph. Come in. *[coming back on stage, followed by Christoph and Traute]* And you must be Traute?
Traute	That's right. *[looking round]* Nice lodgings.
Alex	Hi.
Christoph	Hello Alex.
Hans	*[To Traute]* You've come to study medicine as well?
Traute	No. I'm taking courses in 'Racial Hygiene'. I want to join the Gestapo when I leave. *[beat; Hans looks in horror at Alex]* It's a joke.
Hans	Someone should have warned me you have a sense of humour.
Christoph	*[To Hans; quietly]* Where's your radio?
Alex	It wouldn't surprise me if half our fellow students were in the Gestapo or the S.S. They're so small-minded.
Christoph	Hans? Where's your radio?
Hans	I haven't got one here.
Traute	Then you haven't heard the news?
Hans	What?
Christoph	There's no more chance of peace.
Alex	What do you mean?
Christoph	Our armies started moving into Poland this morning. Now it's definite. There's going to be war with Britain and France.

1940. *The living-room of the Scholls' house.*

Werner is reading a newspaper. Sophie is writing a letter at the table. Magdalene is darning some socks.

Werner   *[Putting down paper]* It's ridiculous! Soon I'll be old enough to leave school and do war service. But I'm not allowed to smoke in public, be on the streets after dark, or even go to a cinema without an adult any more.

Sophie   *[Looking up]* What's that?

Werner   A new directive. There's a long list of things young people mustn't do. *[sarcastically]* Although we'll still be able to join the army and die for the Fatherland, of course.

Magdalene   Don't say that, Werner! Perhaps it'll fizzle out before it goes too far. We've been at war for months and nothing much is happening.

Werner   Then why has Hans been called back into the army?

Sophie   And Ernst. And Fritz.

Magdalene   Please God there won't be any more fighting.

Werner   *[Throws down paper]* I've a good mind to wait till it's dark, then go to the cinema on my own. And smoke one of father's biggest cigars in the front row.

Magdalene   No, Werner.

Werner   That'd show them.

Magdalene   We can't play with the Gestapo. Things are moving beyond curfews and telling people not to smoke. I heard something awful today. *[stops, unsure whether to continue]*

Sophie   Mother?

Magdalene   *[Looks round nervously]* I met a nurse I used to work with this morning. She works at the Children's Home. She says she's desperate to leave. She can't stand it any more.

Sophie	Why not?
Magdalene	The black trucks.
Werner	What?
Magdalene	S.S. lorries. They come to the home from time to time. To take away the children with the greatest disabilities.
Sophie	What for?
Magdalene	At first the nurses were told it's to give them special treatment. But it's much worse than that.
Werner	What happens to them?
Magdalene	They don't come back. *[beat]* They're killed.
Sophie	*[In disbelief]* No!
Magdalene	They're considered completely worthless.
Sophie	That's wicked if it's true.
Magdalene	It's meant to be secret, but so many doctors, nurses and drivers know … Word is spreading.
Werner	Who kills the children?
Magdalene	The S.S. The rumour is, some kind of gas is used in the trucks.
Sophie	*[Stunned]* Surely it's not possible?
Magdalene	My friend says there was a directive from the Führer himself. Incurable patients are to be 'granted release by euthanasia'. Those are the weasel words he uses to describe murder. 'Granted release'.

Werner, Sophie and Magdalene look at each other in despair.

| Sophie | *[Furious]* Why doesn't somebody do something! |

They go off.

48

SCENE 15

Spring 1942. The street outside the Scholls' house.

Robert comes on with Hans, who is wearing an army uniform.

Robert	Your mother and sisters will be so pleased to see you, Hans.
Hans	My regiment have only given me a couple of days. Then it's back to my studies.
Robert	It can't be easy, always switching between the army and university.
Hans	That's how it is for us students. And at least I've only been serving in France, not in the east.
Robert	These hoodlums said we won a total victory as soon as we invaded Russia. So why do they keep sending in more troops?
Hans	Because they're liars, father. I've heard such dreadful things about what's happening in Poland and Russia. You were right about the Nazis from the very beginning. I should have listened.
Robert	*[Lightly]* Why? I never listened to my father. And you saw through them soon enough.
Hans	I wish it had been sooner. Now, in a way, I'm working for them. We don't have enough doctors, so I've been helping out with every operation.
Robert	Good experience, I suppose.
Hans	So many patients die. French and German. *[beat]* What if it's too late to stop Hitler taking over the whole of Europe?
Robert	That frightens me too.
Hans	At least the communists tried to fight him when he came to power. Even if they didn't get very far.
Robert	Most of the socialists I know are in labour camps now. Or dead.

Hans	What will the rest of us say afterwards, if we don't do something? How will we live with our consciences?
Robert	All we can do, is be true to ourselves.
Hans	And to God. *[beat]* Whenever I have any free time from duty, I walk with Alex in the woods. I write to dear Rose. I read poetry and philosophy. I try to make sense of this senseless war. But it's not enough. I feel cut off from life. From God. From myself.
Robert	You're very tired, Hans.
Hans	It's not me, father. It's our country that needs waking up.

Robert puts his arm round Hans as they go off.

● ●

SCENE 16

Spring 1942. The living-room of the Scholls' house.

Inge is sitting, reading a letter. Sophie is standing behind her.

Sophie	How's Ernst?
Inge	Alive. That's the main thing.
Sophie	Is that all he says?
Inge	You know how much soldiers' letters are censored. But he sends his love to everybody. Including you.
Sophie	That's nice.
Inge	Still nothing from Fritz?
Sophie	Not for over two weeks. Letters take so long to come back from Russia. I'm worried.
Inge	That he's been wounded?
Sophie	Not only that. I've seen so little of him, since the war started. I don't know how much of my real feelings to show in a letter.

Inge	Do you love him?
Sophie	The time we spent together feels like a dream. I loved him when I was dreaming. But now?
Inge	You'll have to make your mind up soon. There'll be any number of boys chasing you when you start at university next month.

Magdalene comes on with Hans.

Magdalene	We've a visitor, girls.
Sophie and Inge	*[Delighted]* Hans!

Hans embraces his sisters.

Hans	Good to see you.
Inge	Still in one piece?
Hans	Just about.
Magdalene	Though he needs feeding up.
Sophie	There's nothing wrong with him. All that French sun's done him good.

Robert comes on, holding a sheet of paper.

Robert	Did this come with the post? There's no envelope.
Magdalene	What is it?
Robert	Something rather odd. A sermon.
Hans	*[Surprised]* A sermon?
Robert	*[Looking at paper]* Given by the bishop of Munster. Bishop Galen. It's been copied privately.
Inge	It isn't an official document?
Robert	*[Reading]* Oh no. It's much better than that. This is a piece of the real truth.
Sophie	What do you mean, father?

Robert	The bishop's speaking out openly against the Nazis. He says if we allow the disabled and the weak to be murdered, then none of us will be safe.
Hans	Can I see? *[he joins **Robert** and they read together]*
Robert	At last! Someone's standing up to them.
Magdalene	But who copied the sermon and sent it here?
Hans	There's no name.
Inge	Whoever did, is risking their life.
Hans	*[Getting excited]* The bishop says the National Socialists are rotting the country. He demands an end to the unlawful actions of the Gestapo and a return to justice!
Magdalene	To hear those words said freely! It's amazing.
Hans	And it's not just us the sermon's been sent to. *[points to paper]* See? It's been hectographed. Maybe there are hundreds of copies. Thousands even.
Robert	Not that a leaflet will make much difference.
Hans	It's a start.
Sophie	It shows we're not alone in hating Hitler.
Magdalene	Will Bishop Galen be arrested?
Robert	He's too popular for even the Nazis to strike down publicly. They'll wait and deal with him when no one's looking.
Inge	Whoever's printing this is taking a big risk. The government would call it treason.
Hans	I call it wonderful. To do so much with a simple copying machine. If only we had one.

SCENE 17

Late spring 1942. The atrium at Munich University.
Jakob Schmid, the caretaker, is brushing the floor.
Students cross the stage in various directions on their way to
lectures. As some of them pass Jakob, they exchange the Nazi
salute with him.
Willi Graf, Alex and Traute look on, and try not to giggle.

Willi	Anyone would think Jakob ran the university, instead of just being the caretaker.
Traute	When the caretaker's such good friends with the Gestapo, it pays to salute.
Alex	Who have we got next?
Traute	Professor Huber.
Willi	Thank heavens for one lecturer who doesn't spout Nazi nonsense all the time.
Traute	Ssh!
Alex	Schmid's got very big ears.
Traute	*[Looking off]* Here they are. Hans has got back from his parents.
Alex	He's been back a couple of days.

Christoph and Hans come on together and walk past Schmid.

Schmid	*[Saluting]* Heil Hitler!
Hans	*[Not saluting]* Good morning, Jakob.
Christoph	*[Not saluting]* Isn't it lovely and sunny?

Schmid scowls at them, then resumes sweeping.

Traute	I thought you were going to be late.
Christoph	Not for Huber.

Hans	Listen! I've heard a great joke – *[notices **Willi** for the first time]* Oh.
Willi	*[Introducing himself]* Willi Graf. I've been attending some of the same lectures as you recently.
Hans	Yes. I've noticed you.
Alex	Stop being suspicious, Hans. Willi is one of us.
Traute	Better than us. He never joined the Hitler Youth. Despite all the threats.
Hans	*[Shaking **Willi's** hand]* Pleased to meet you, Willi. I'm Hans Scholl.
Willi	Hello.
Christoph	And I'm Christoph Probst.
Willi	*[Shakes **Christoph's** hand]* Hi.
Alex	*[To **Willi**]* I told you there were a few sane students amongst all the idiots.
Traute	Now, what was this joke?
Hans	OK. You know the Ministry of Propaganda says that every German should be honest, intelligent and a National Socialist?
Traute	Goebbels won't shut up about it.
Hans	So why's it impossible?
Alex	Go on.
Hans	If you're intelligent and a Nazi, you can't be honest. If you're honest and a Nazi, you can't be intelligent. And if you're honest and intelligent, you can't be a Nazi.
	The others laugh.
Traute	*[Looking towards **Schmid**]* Ssh!
Willi	Unfortunately that's not a joke. It's the plain truth.
Christoph	Time we were listening to old man Huber.

Traute	Sure. *[moving off]* Where are we having lunch afterwards?
Willi	*[Going off]* Do you know the 'Bodega'? It's cheap and good.
Christoph	*[Going off]* Don't talk about food. I'm starving.
	*Alex takes hold of **Hans's** arm to hold him back.*
Alex	*[Quietly]* Wait a minute. *[he checks to see that **Schmid** isn't taking any notice]* You know we talked about drawing up a leaflet, like Bishop Galen?
Hans	Have you had some luck?
Alex	I've bought a cheap typewriter and a little copying machine.
Hans	You're a genius, Alex!
Alex	It's taken every pfennig I've been able to scrounge from home.
Hans	You haven't said anything to the others?
Alex	Not yet. We can write and print the leaflet ourselves. But we'll need help to distribute them. Traute? Willi?
Hans	Maybe.
Alex	Christoph?
Hans	Definitely not. He's got a young family to think of. And we're about to do something very dangerous, Alex. We're going to start telling the truth.
Christoph	*[Comes back on]* What's holding you up?
Hans	Nothing.
Alex	On our way.
	***Hans** and **Alex** follow **Christoph** off. **Schmid** goes off in the opposite direction.*

SCENE 18

22 February 1943. The open area.

Reichhart comes on, with a perfectly tied bow-tie. He is followed by the Assistant.

Reichhart	Until then the poison had just been in Hans Scholl's head. Now it started to ooze out onto paper. 'Leaflets of the White Rose' he called the dreadful scribblings he produced with Alex Schmorell.
Assistant	Why the 'White Rose'?
Reichhart	Who knows? Hans had a girlfriend called Rose. And sometimes, in the army, he kept a rosebud in his uniform pocket.
Assistant	*[Appalled]* What?
Reichhart	He admitted it in a letter the investigators found. He said you should always carry a little secret with you, when you are surrounded by National Socialists.
Assistant	Perhaps a white rose symbolizes truth and beauty.
Reichhart	Only to a lunatic!

The Chorus enter at various points on the stage.

Assistant	Such wicked things he and Alex wrote in their leaflets.
Chorus 1	'Every honest German feels ashamed of his government.'
Reichhart	*[Horrified]* Then to spread these lies around.
Chorus 2	'Use passive resistance to stop the spread of this godless war machine.'
Assistant	Soon the leaflets were appearing in Munich and a few other towns.
Reichhart	And then a second leaflet was written!
Chorus 3	'Since the conquest of Poland, three hundred thousand Jews have been brutally murdered.'

Reichhart	And a third and a fourth! Didn't these traitors realize their pernicious filth was undermining the war effort?
Chorus 4	'Every opponent of National Socialism must use sabotage in armament factories, in all the war industries and in the newspapers.'
Assistant	Unimaginable evil to call for sabotage!
Reichhart	We didn't know who was producing this sewage, but we knew they were the worst kind of traitors.
Assistant	The police wanted to find and stop them.
Reichhart	But all the time, the leaflets were spreading. Dozens were sent anonymously in the post.
Assistant	To teachers, priests, pub owners.
Reichhart	Anyone who could influence public opinion.
Chorus 5	'We must attack the power of Adolf Hitler.'
Reichhart	They even had the nerve to twist and turn the words of our greatest writers.
Chorus 6	'The unfamiliar word "freedom" is murmured on every lip . . .'
Chorus 7	'. . . until on the steps of the temple, we cry out in delight . . .'
Chorus (All)	"Freedom! Freedom!"'
Reichhart	Who's responsible for this filth? That's what everyone asked. Who? Who? Who?
Chorus (All)	'We are your bad conscience. We will not be silent. The White Rose will not leave you in peace.'
Reichhart	*[Furious]* Shut up! Shut up! Shut up!
	*The **Chorus** goes off silently.*
Assistant	*[Frightened by **Reichhart's** outburst]* Are you all right, Johann? Do you want me to fetch you a glass of water? *[beat]* Will you be able to perform if you're needed?

Reichhart	*[Completely calm again]* The tie is good, but the collar feels wrinkled.
Assistant	Only a little.
Reichhart	Then find me another one!
Assistant	Of course, Johann. *[going off]* Straight away.

Reichhart follows the *Assistant* off.

• •

SCENE 19

June 1942. The atrium at Munich University.

Students come on and gather in groups around the stage. *Alex*, *Christoph* and *Willi* come on and talk together in one corner as *Professor Huber*, who has a strong limp, comes on.

Alex	Good morning, Professor Huber.
Huber	*[Stops for a moment]* Good morning boys. Ready for a little philosophy this morning?
Christoph	What are we doing, sir?
Huber	Leibniz. *[quietly]* Whether an individual should do what the state tells him is right. Or follow his own conscience.
Willi	I look forward to it.
Huber	I'll see you all in the lecture hall.

*He resumes walking across the stage. **Student 1** starts following him, imitating his limp for the amusement of **Students 2** and **3**.*

Alex	*[Angrily]* Hey!

Alex moves to stop *Student 1*, but *Willi* grabs his arm.

Willi	*[Quietly]* No, Alex. We mustn't draw attention to ourselves. *[points as **Schmid** comes on stage]* Especially not now.

*Various students, including **Students 1**, 2 and 3 give the Nazi salute. **Schmid** walks angrily up a set of steps in the atrium and holds up a handful of leaflets.*

Schmid	Your attention! Everyone! Attention! *[the students all turn to listen; **Sophie** and **Traute** come on]* Some of you may have heard of the vile, unpatriotic leaflets that have been appearing in local towns. Today I found some of this so-called 'White Rose' filth in one of the lecture rooms. I have informed the university chancellor. Doctor Wüst tells me that he will not let Munich University have its name tarnished by the presence of such garbage. Let us be clear. If any student is in any way involved in the production or distribution of this madness, they will be found and punished. Most severely! You have been warned.
	Schmid goes off angrily, exchanging Nazi salutes with one or two students as he does so.
Traute	*[Looks round before speaking]* Are you getting used to the craziness of university life, Sophie?
Sophie	I've only been here a month and it just keeps getting stranger.
Christoph	*[Calls]* Traute! Are you ignoring us?
Traute	I didn't see you, Christoph. *[to **Sophie**]* Come on.
	Traute and Sophie join the boys.
Alex	Good afternoon, Traute.
Traute	Hello, Alex.
Alex	Willi, have you met Hans's little sister, Sophie, yet?
Sophie	Hey! I'm not so little.
Willi	*[Shakes hands with **Sophie**]* Delighted to meet you.
Traute	She joined us in May.
Christoph	What do you think of studying here?
Sophie	It's better than war service.
Traute	For sure.
Willi	What were you doing?

Sophie	Looking after the children of factory workers. My boss was 'a hundred and fifty percent Nazi', if you know what I mean.
Christoph	Only too well.
Alex	The university's full of them, unfortunately.
Sophie	That's why it's so good to see these leaflets Schmid was talking about. *[takes out a leaflet]* Have you read one yet?
Alex	*[Shocked]* Put it away!
Willi	Immediately!
Sophie	*[Puts leaflet away]* I found it in the library. I only wanted to know who's writing such marvellous things.
Willi	You're not the only one, Sophie.
Traute	It's what the local police want more than anything.
Christoph	*[Innocently]* I've read a couple of them. It's astonishing. They sound just like the discussions we have with Hans sometimes –
Willi	*[Hurriedly]* Lots of people speak like that. The 'White Rose' could be anyone.
Traute	From a different town, probably. Nothing to do with Hans. Or any of us.
Christoph	*[Puzzled]* Of course not.
Alex	Where is your brother, anyway? We've got an anatomy lecture in a minute.
Sophie	I don't know. I haven't seen him today.
Willi	He's going to be late.
Traute	*[Looking off]* Here he comes.
	The other students start going off to lectures.
Hans	*[Coming on]* What are you all waiting for?
Alex	You, slowcoach.
Hans	Hi, Sophie. Have you got a lecture this afternoon?

Sophie	No. I'm finished for the day.
Traute	Lucky you.
Hans	What are you going to do?
Sophie	I don't know. Maybe write to Fritz. I owe him a long letter.
Hans	If you've nothing else planned, why not write your letter at my apartment? Then we can eat together this evening.
Sophie	OK.
Alex	*[To Hans]* Come on. *[goes off]*
Traute	*[Going off]* We're going to be late.
Hans	*[To Sophie]* See you later, Sophie. *[goes off]*
Sophie	Bye.
Christoph	*[Going off]* See you.
Willi	*[Going off]* See you.

When Sophie is alone on stage, she takes out the White Rose leaflet again.

• •

SCENE 20

Later that day, June 1942; and 22 February 1943.

Hans's lodgings. There is a desk covered in books and a chair.

Reichhart and the Assistant come on, and climb up so they can look down on the apartment.

Assistant	June nineteen forty-two. Going to Hans's apartment was the fatal mistake.
Reichhart	That's when the venom finally entered Sophie Scholl's bloodstream as well.
Assistant	And such a deadly venom.

Sophie comes on, with a notepad and pen. She looks at the desk, clears a space on it and sits down to write a letter.

Sophie   *[Starts to write]* 'Dear Fritz'– *[stops writing; pause]* What's next? I could tell you about the walk I took in the English Garden yesterday. How the evening sun shone through the tops of the trees. The birds sang. Everything was peaceful and in harmony. Except for us humans, of course. If I think about what we are doing to each other, I'll go mad. *[throws down pen]* I can't put such depressing nonsense in a letter, can I, poor Fritz?

Fed up, she looks idly at the books on the desk, then picks one up which is half open. She starts to read. Then she takes out the White Rose leaflet and compares it with the book. Quietly she reads aloud.

'The unfamiliar word "freedom" is murmured on every lip, until, on the steps of the temple, we cry out in delight, "Freedom! Freedom!".'

Hans   *[Coming in with a brown paper bag]* I've bought some bread and cheese. I said we'd meet up with Alex and Traute at the 'Lombardi' later.

Sophie   *[Getting up]* Hans … *[she holds up the leaflet]* You've written these, haven't you? The White Rose leaflets?

Hans	*[Evasive]* What makes you say that?
Sophie	There's a quote in this one from Goethe. Your copy of Goethe is open on the desk.
Hans	So what? Everybody reads him.
Sophie	You've marked the very same passage that's in the leaflet. About freedom. Hans, I'm not a fool. I remember you reading Bishop Galen's sermon. Afterwards, you said you wanted a copying machine.
Hans	It's dangerous to know about these things, Sophie.
Sophie	Are you working alone?
Hans	You'd better forget what you've seen.
Sophie	*[Insistent]* Are you on your own, Hans?
Hans	There are a few of us. Two or three, that's all. We write and print the leaflets in a friend's studio.
Sophie	Then I must help you.
Hans	No.
Sophie	I must and I will.
Hans	But Sophie –
Sophie	*[Over]* I have never been so proud of you. We are crushed beneath a godless evil in this country. No one dares speak of it on the streets. There's a silence in the universities; in the barracks and the bars. But you have found the courage to speak. Do you think my conscience can be stilled? That's not what our parents taught us.
Hans	*[Lightly]* Be true to yourself and to God. Whatever anyone else says.
Sophie	Then, please, don't condemn me to silence, Hans. Let me speak too. I want to be part of the 'White Rose'.
	Blackout.

ACT 2

July 1942. Eickemeyer's basement.

Alex is turning the handle on a small duplicator. *Hans* takes one completed leaflet at a time from the duplicator, folds it neatly and puts it into an envelope. *Willi* takes an address from a phone directory and writes it on the envelope. They work rhythmically and silently.

The *Chorus* and the *Voice of Radio* address the audience.

Chorus	Attention! Attention! Please stand by.
VoR	July 1942. Excellent news from the Atlantic. Our U-boat fleet continues to devastate the British and American war machine. Seven hundred thousand tons of shipping has been sunk in the last month.
Chorus	Attention! Attention! Please stand by.

VoR	In the east, our great summer push is meeting with unparalleled success. The Russian army is in full retreat between the Donets and Don rivers.
Chorus	Attention! Attention! Please stand by.
VoR	The enemy are now falling back towards Stalingrad. But even that great city won't protect them for long from our brave and determined soldiers. Victory for the Fatherland is assured. Heil Hitler!
Chorus	*[In a fading chant]* Attention! Attention! Please stand by. Attention! Attention! Please stand by. Attention! Attention! Please stand by.

The Voice of Radio goes off, together with the Chorus.

Alex stops turning the handle and rubs his arm.

Alex	Can we please stop for five minutes?
Hans	We've only done forty so far.
Alex	We won't do much more if my arm drops off.
Willi	Anyone would think we're alcoholics. *[reads out addresses on envelopes]* 'The Golden Bear Tavern' . . . 'The Augsburg Inn'.
Hans	What better place to send leaflets to?
Alex	Get the landlord thinking and maybe he'll say something to his customers.
Willi	Let's hope so.
Hans	Do you want to swap round, Alex? *[teasing]* If you haven't got the strength for the job.
Alex	See what *your* muscles are like after half an hour of this rusty old handle.

Sophie and Traute come in.

Sophie	We've got them! *[holds up a handful of stamps]*
Traute	Two hundred, eight-pfennig stamps. *[holds up stamps]*

ACT 2 SCENE 1

Alex	Well done!
Hans	Where did you buy them?
Sophie	Don't worry. We split up and went to twenty different places.
Traute	Never more than ten stamps at a time.
Sophie	I said it was for wedding invitations.
Traute	I said it was for news of a funeral.
Sophie	And then we met Christoph.
Traute	We're all having a picnic with him and Herta in the English Garden.
Willi	When?
Sophie	In about an hour.
Hans	*[Annoyed]* But we're spending the whole weekend printing. We agreed to forget our friends and our studies.
Alex	We've got to eat sometime. A picnic sounds good.
Hans	Well –
Sophie	*[Over]* We promised we'd go.
Traute	We had to. Christoph says he's got some important news for us.
Willi	What about?
Traute	He wouldn't say.
Sophie	He wants to tell us all together. He was going to come here to do it otherwise.
Traute	We had a real job, shaking him off.
Alex	You did the right thing.
Hans	He mustn't know anything about this place.
Sophie	I think he's getting suspicious about what we're doing all the time.

Hans	'Suspicious' is fine. As long as he doesn't actually know what we're up to, he's safe.
Willi	Well, if we've only got another hour, one of you ladies will have to volunteer for a horrible job.
Traute	What's that?
Willi	Putting the stamps on. I can't stand the taste of gum.
Sophie	I don't mind.
Hans	Are you sure? With Hitler on the front, it means you're going to have to keep kissing his backside.
Sophie	Fine. *[she sticks a stamp on one envelope]* Because one day – to use my favourite local expression – Hitler can kiss all our arses!
	They all go off.

SCENE 2

An hour later. The English Park in Munich.

Herta carries on a small picnic basket and sits down. Christoph backs onto the stage, unreeling some string which is attached to something offstage.

Christoph	*[Looping the free end of the string round his fingers]* There. That should keep it cool.
Herta	As long as the water doesn't get in.
Christoph	It'll be fine.
Herta	It was nice of your step-mother to give it to us.
Christoph	She's more pleased than anyone, Herta. She knows we want to celebrate with our friends.
Herta	*[Waving off]* There's Sophie.
Christoph	*[Looking off]* They're all here.
	Hans, Sophie, Traute, Willi and Alex come on.

67

Hans	Hi.
Sophie	Hiya.
Christoph	Come and sit down. The grass is dry.
Traute	*[Greets **Herta** with a hug]* Where are the boys, Herta?
Herta	With my mother.
	***Hans**, **Sophie** and the rest find places to sit down.*
Alex	Good to see you. Especially if you've brought some nice food.
Christoph	Better than just food. *[he holds up the string]*
Willi	*[Looking off at the end of the string]* There's something interesting cooling in the pond.
Christoph	We'll open it in a minute.
Herta	You look like you haven't seen the sun for days, Hans.
Christoph	You're all very pale and pasty.
Herta	What have you been up to?
Hans	*[Slightly awkwardly]* You know. Studying.
Herta	Really?
Alex	Yes.
Sophie	*[Deliberately changing the subject]* What's the news you've got for us?
Traute	Come on. We've waited long enough.
Herta	Go on, Christoph. You tell them.
Christoph	*[To **Herta**]* It's your news really. But wait a moment. *[he reels in the string, which is attached to a dripping wet bottle of wine]* We've got to celebrate properly.
Willi	I've got a corkscrew on my knife.
Christoph	*[Handing him the bottle]* Then be my guest.
	***Willi** opens the wine under:*

Sophie	So, what is it, Herta?
Herta	Well, I'm afraid you're going to have another birthday to remember soon.
Alex	Eh?
Traute	Do you mean . . .?
Herta	Yes! We waited till I was certain. I'm pregnant again.
Traute	How wonderful!
Sophie	Congratulations! Both of you!
Willi	That's great.
Hans	Well done!
Alex	Twenty-two years old and your third child! No wonder you're always looking tired, Christoph.
	Everyone laughs. **Willi** *holds the bottle up.*
Willi	Do we have any glasses?
Herta	Here.
	She opens the picnic basket and hands round glasses. **Willi** *pours wine into them under:*
Hans	It makes such a nice change to hear good news for once.
Christoph	We knew you'd be pleased.
Sophie	When's it due?
Herta	Next January.
Sophie	I'm so happy for you. Babies are wonderful.
Alex	They're noisy and messy.
Sophie	They're divine. Even when they're tiny, you can see exactly who they're going to become.
Traute	She won't stop talking about the ones she looked after during her war service.

Herta	*[Teasing]* Well, who knows, Sophie? When the war's over and you marry Fritz –
Sophie	*[Embarrassed]* Phooey!
Willi	Has everyone got a glass?
Sophie	*[To **Herta**]* No one's talking about marriage!
Alex	*[To **Willi**]* Yes. And I'm dying of thirst.
Willi	*[Raises his glass]* Then to Christoph and Herta.
Sophie, Hans Traute, Alex, and **Willi**	Christoph and Herta!
Alex	And the latest addition to their family.
Sophie	Absolutely.
Christoph	Thank you very much.
Herta	Now help yourselves to sandwiches.
	The others help themselves to sandwiches from the picnic basket through the rest of the scene.
Hans	And I've something for you Herta. *[he takes a rosebud from his pocket and gives it to her]*
Herta	Thank you, Hans. Do you always keep a rosebud in your pocket?
Alex	*[Joking]* Doesn't everybody?
Hans	I love roses. They're special when they're buds. *[points to the rosebud]* Like your baby, it's full of what it's going to become. In time it opens and blooms. It fills a room with its scent.
Christoph	Babies do that, for sure.
	The others laugh.
Hans	And even when it fades, you remember what a rose was like. Its beauty lasts a long time.

Traute	*[Teasing]* How strong is this wine?
Sophie	Forgive my brother. He's been working too hard and getting no sleep. That's why he's talking like a poet.
Herta	What exactly is it you're so busy studying? Christoph hasn't been working that hard.
Hans	Sophie's exaggerating.
Herta	According to Christoph, you all disappear as soon as lectures finish. It sounds like you're up to something.
Brownshirt	*[Offstage]* No! No! No!

*A **Jewish man**, with a gold star of David on his jacket, hurries on, followed by the **Brownshirt**. The **Brownshirt** points to the other side of the stage.*

Go back out! The park isn't for your sort. Never use it as a shortcut again.

*The **Jewish man** goes off. The **Brownshirt** turns to the group of friends.*

Disgusting, the liberties these people take, isn't it? I'll be glad when the last of them have been pushed out of Munich. Well, it's a nice day. Enjoy your picnic.

*He goes off. **Hans, Sophie, Traute, Alex, Willi, Herta** and **Christoph** grimace and shrug at each other.*

Herta	It makes me so mad.
Christoph	Don't get upset, Herta.
Traute	No, you mustn't. It's not good for you or the baby.
Herta	But it's so unfair.
Sophie	*[Trying to distract **Herta**]* Have you thought of any names yet?
Herta	Yes. But the guys'll just laugh.
Traute	Then tell us in secret.
Sophie	Yes. Go on.

Sophie and Traute huddle round Herta. They have a whispered conversation about names, as Christoph casually moves away from his wife to speak privately with Hans, Alex and Willi.

Christoph	You know the one thing I don't like about being a father again?
Alex	The nappies?
Christoph	*[Looks over his shoulder first]* The thought of bringing up children in a world run by idiots like that.
Hans	Perhaps they won't be round for much longer.
Willi	*[Looks over his shoulder]* Hitler's bound to run out of luck. He can't go on winning everywhere.
Christoph	I'm not so sure. I believe everything has a purpose. We're on this earth to move towards good, not evil. But, right now, it seems everything is going the other way.
Alex	Things will change. Willi's right.
Christoph	We have to make them change. *[quietly]* That's why I want to join the White Rose.
Willi	*[Beat]* What are you talking about, Christoph? The sun and the wine must have got to you.
Christoph	I know it's you lot writing the leaflets. I've known for some time. It's the style. The quotations. There's no one else it could be.
Hans	Please don't say any more, Christoph.
Christoph	I want to help. It's my duty.

Herta, Sophie and Traute burst out laughing.

Herta	*[Amused]* No! 'Bertram' and 'Baldwin' are too serious if my little baby is a boy.
Traute	Ssh! Ssh! Ssh! They're listening.

The girls resume talking quietly.

Hans	[*Quietly to* **Christoph**] Your first duty is to your wife and family.
Christoph	But I want to do something.
Alex	Hans is right. You've got other responsibilities.
Willi	We're all single. We can take risks.
Hans	And you're a great help already.
Christoph	I don't see how.
Hans	The discussions we have. About right and wrong.
Willi	It's vital. Talking honestly with you, and one or two others. That's the oxygen that lets our minds breathe.
Christoph	But that's nothing.
Alex	Christoph, if you got involved and the Gestapo ever found out –
Hans	They wouldn't just hurt *you*.
Christoph	[*Beat. Looks at* **Herta,** *then nods to* **Hans**] I know. But it's so frustrating.
Hans	You're playing your part by discussing ideas with us.
Christoph	I've been thinking a lot since the first leaflets appeared. Maybe we can talk some time about other things you should say.
Alex	That would be good.
Herta	[*Getting up*] Christoph, I'm afraid I promised mother we'd pick the children up by two.
Christoph	Oh. We'd better get going then.
	Sophie *and* **Traute** *collect all the empty wine glasses and put them in the picnic basket.*
Alex	Thanks very much for the wine and food.
Willi	And the good news.
Herta	You can all come to my mother's if you like.

Sophie	*[Reluctant]* That'd be nice Herta, but –
Traute	We've got essays to catch up on. That kind of thing.
Herta	You're right, Christoph. They are hard workers.
Christoph	Well, just remember. If there's any way I can help with your 'studies'.
Hans	Don't worry. I'm sure there will be, one day.
	They all go off.

• •

SCENE 3

22 February 1943. The open area.

Reichhart *comes on. The* **Assistant** *follows, carefully brushing a top hat throughout the scene.*

Reichhart	Studying! Printing subversive trash, more likely! Can you believe it? An architect gave those damned students the use of his studio.
Assistant	Perhaps he didn't know what they were doing.
Reichhart	Of course he knew! It was the same in other cities. Like Hamburg and Berlin. Little gangs of rats, hiding in basements. Whispering against the Führer.

Assistant	Absolute insanity!
Reichhart	Of course it was!
Assistant	We were winning everywhere, when the first leaflets appeared. We were hammering the British in North Africa. The Soviet Union seemed bound to collapse.
Reichhart	Victory was close enough for us to stroke its skin.
Assistant	What a strange time to attack the Führer. Now, perhaps, when everything's starting to go wrong, it makes sense –
Reichhart	*[Gives a warning cough]*
Assistant	*[Looks round nervously]* Sorry, Johann. *[quietly]* All I'm saying is they must actually have meant it.
Reichhart	I'm afraid they did. And no wonder, given the dreadful backgrounds they came from. Especially the Scholls. It seems criminal they weren't found and arrested immediately.
Assistant	*[Offering **Reichhart** the hat]* Want to try it on?
Reichhart	*[Taking hat]* But if the police weren't very smart in discovering what Hans and Sophie were up to, at least they sprang a nice surprise on the rest of the Scholls. *[puts on hat]*
Assistant	*[Takes out hand mirror and holds it up for **Reichhart** to look at]* Well, Johann?
Reichhart	Not bad. Almost ready to wear. *[takes off hat and holds it out to **Assistant**]* Once you've given it a good brush.
	*Reichhart goes off, followed by the **Assistant**, who angrily resumes brushing the hat.*

SCENE 4

July 1942. The living-room of the Scholls' house.

Robert is working on some accounts at the table. Magdalene comes in.

Magdalene	Robert. Two men to see you. *[Gestapo 1 and 2 come in]* I won't say 'gentlemen'.
Gestapo 1	I'm not surprised to be meeting you again, Mr Scholl.
Robert	What do you want?
Gestapo 2	You must come with us. A serious accusation has been made.
Robert	What accusation?
Gestapo 1	That you have spoken out publicly against the government.
Magdalene	Nonsense! My husband wouldn't dream of it.
Robert	*[Warning his wife to be cautious]* Magdalene.
Magdalene	Some business rival – another accountant – must have dreamt this up.
Gestapo 1	A young woman working in your father's office brought the matter to our attention.
Gestapo 2	She said her conscience forced her to do so. Even though, personally, she likes you very much.
Robert	And what am I supposed to have said?
Gestapo 2	That Hitler is God's curse on mankind.
Gestapo 1	Do you deny it?
Robert	*[Sighs]* How can anyone deny the simple truth?

Robert goes off with Gestapo 1 and 2, followed by Magdalene.

SCENE 5

Late July 1942. The atrium at Munich University.

Schmid is cleaning a stretch of wall. Students drift on in informal groups. Sophie and Professor Huber come on from different directions and meet.

Huber	Ah, Sophie.
Sophie	Hello, Professor Huber.
Huber	Looking forward to the summer vacation?
Sophie	Not really. I've got more war service.
Huber	What are you doing?
Sophie	Two months' work in an ammunition factory.
Huber	Poor you. And ... er ... *[looks around before speaking quietly]* Any news of your father?
Sophie	*[Surprised]* You've heard he was arrested?
Huber	Hans told me.

Hans, Alex and Willi come on and go to join Sophie and Huber.

Sophie	*[Quietly to Huber]* His trial's next month. We're all very worried.
Huber	Of course.
Hans	Hi! Are you busy tonight, Professor?
Huber	The end of term's always busy. Why?
Hans	We're having a party.
Alex	Our last chance to celebrate before rejoining our units.
Willi	The army's sending us to Russia for our summer holidays.
Alex	*[Sarcastically]* Isn't that kind of them?
Huber	You don't want an old man like me at a party.

Sophie	We'd love you to be there.
Hans	It's not your age, but your ideas that matter. You're not afraid to think for yourself. *[looks round]* If you know what I mean.
Huber	If you're sure, I'd be delighted to come.
Willi	Eickemeyer's studio.
Alex	At nine o'clock.
Huber	I'll see you there. *[starts moving off]*
Hans	Oh. And Professor –
Huber	Don't worry. I'll bring something nice to drink. *[he goes off]*
Alex	Thanks.
Sophie	I thought the party was starting at eight.
Hans	A little later now. Do you mind helping Traute prepare for it?
Sophie	Not at all.
Hans	Good. We've something else to do first. Alex has just had an excellent idea.

*Everyone except **Hans** goes off.*

SCENE 6

That evening. Outside Munich University.

***Hans** looks round very carefully, then signals off stage.*

Hans	*[Calls softly]* OK. Quick.

***Alex** and **Willi** come on, carrying brushes and a pot of paint. They all speak cautiously during the rest of the scene.*

Alex	*[Quietly]* There's only enough paint for one more slogan.
Hans	Here's as good as anywhere.
Willi	Mustn't leave the university out.
Alex	*[Dipping a brush in the paint]* Keep watch, Hans.

Willi	If anyone comes along –
Hans	*[Clenching his fists]* Don't worry. I know how to handle Nazi thugs.
	*Hans keeps watch as **Alex** and **Willi** begin to paint 'Long Live Freedom' on the wall. All three continue with the graffiti as:*

● ●

SCENE 7

The same evening. Eickemeyer's basement.

All the printing equipment has been covered up.
***Huber, Traute** and **Christoph** are standing and drinking wine together. **Herta** is sitting next to them. Music plays softly in the background throughout.*

Huber	You're not going to Russia with the others then, Christoph?
Christoph	Not yet.
Herta	His unit is sure to be sent later.
Traute	It's a shame he can't wait till the baby comes.
Herta	That's months away yet.
Christoph	I wish I could stay though. *[puts his hand protectively on **Herta**]* It's not been so easy this time, has it?
Herta	I'm fine.
Huber	To listen to the radio, you'd think the war in Russia was over long ago.
	***Sophie** comes on.*
Herta	Where's your brother got to? And Willi and Alex?
Sophie	*[Evasive]* I'm not sure.
Traute	Sophie and Hans already have a brother in Russia.
Huber	I didn't know that.

ACT 2 SCENE 7

Sophie	Werner. He's the youngest in the family. He's serving at a casualty station.
Herta	Poor Sophie's really suffering. Her boyfriend's been sent there as well.
Huber	The campaign's a complete misjudgement.
Christoph	I agree.
Sophie	Fritz's letters feel like they're coming from a spiritual desert.
Huber	The whole war's a sickness. But at last people are beginning to protest. *[takes leaflet from pocket]* Have you seen this? It's by a group calling itself the 'White Rose'. I found it lying on a table in a café.
	Sophie, Christoph and Traute exchange worried glances.
Sophie	I've heard of the White Rose, Professor. But I don't know anything about them.
Traute	*[Takes Huber's glass]* Let's get you some more wine.
Huber	Thank you. Perhaps a drop.
	Traute goes to top up the glass.
Herta	Sophie? What's your brother up to? It's a strange party, when the host doesn't appear.
	Willi, Alex and Hans leave the completed slogan and go off stage.
Sophie	He'll be here any minute.
Herta	But where's he got to?
Traute	*[Returns with Huber's glass]* There you are.
Huber	*[Takes glass]* Thanks. *[to Sophie]* Yes. Where are the rest? I was looking forward to talking to them.
Herta	Alex never misses a party.
Sophie	*[Awkwardly]* I don't know where they've got to.

Traute	*[Deliberately changing the subject]* Have you told everyone about your dream, Sophie?
Sophie	Oh, no.
Christoph	What's that?
Sophie	A silly little thing I had last night.
Herta	Well, go on. Tell us.
Sophie	All right ... I was out walking in the country with Hans and Alex. Our arms were linked and they were swinging me off the ground, so I half-skipped and half-walked. It was a cloudy, muggy day and we were talking about the need for fresh air.
Christoph	Your bedroom must have been too stuffy.
Sophie	And Hans said that God sometimes sends us a mouthful of his own breath. Then the strangest thing happened.
Herta	What?
Sophie	Hans looked up and blew out an enormous, bright blue jet of air. It went right up to the sky, blowing all the gloomy clouds away. Until the whole of the sky was completely blue.
Christoph	You're right. It is a strange dream.
Traute	I think it's beautiful.
Herta	So do I.
Huber	Too many anatomy lectures about blood and oxygen.
	The others laugh.
	Hans, Alex and **Willi** *hurry on.*
Hans	Sorry we're late.
Alex	Hello Professor.
Willi	I hope you've left some wine for us.
Herta	What have you boys been up to?
Hans	*[Making up an excuse]* There's ... some trouble with the trams.

Alex	Where's this lovely wine?
Traute	I'll get you some.

*Alex follows **Traute**, who pours wine for the newcomers. **Sophie** brings a chair to join **Herta**.*

Sophie	Do you ever have unusual dreams?
Herta	Well . . .

Herta and Sophie converse quietly, as do Alex and Traute. Huber starts a quiet conversation with Hans, as Christoph goes up to Willi.

Christoph	*[Discreetly]* I see you've given up medicine, to become a decorator.
Willi	*[Puzzled]* Pardon?
Christoph	You've a streak of paint on your hand.
Willi	Oh. Thanks. *[he wipes off the paint with a handkerchief]*
Christoph	*[Quietly]* I think painting slogans is stupid. It's dangerous and it doesn't change anything.
Willi	You haven't seen any paint. And we've been here all evening.

*Willi goes to get some wine and talks with **Alex** and **Traute**, as **Christoph** joins **Herta** and **Sophie**.*

Huber	*[To **Hans**; he takes out leaflet]* I was talking to your friends about this a little earlier. The White Rose.
Hans	*[Surprised, but then recovers]* Oh yes. I've seen one or two leaflets. They're so badly written.
Huber	Perhaps they could be improved a little. But the thinking behind them is absolutely right. We must always try to resist evil.

Huber and Hans look carefully at each other for a moment.

Hans	*[Cautiously]* Even when it controls every little part of our lives?

Huber	Especially then! Look at me. I've limped since I was a child. If I was born like this now, I'd probably be killed.
Hans	Yes. I've heard what happens in the hospitals.
Huber	I'd far rather have a crippled leg than a crippled soul. But that's what's happening to Germany. We've caught a terrible disease.
Hans	I couldn't agree more.
Huber	If we want to stop the cancer spreading even further, it's time for action, not words.
Herta	*[Gets up]* If there's trouble with the trams . . .
Christoph	Yes. We'd better go back to your mother's.
Sophie	I hope the children have given her some peace.
Huber	*[Reluctantly]* Perhaps it's time I was going too. My wife'll be worrying about me. *[quietly to **Hans**]* Maybe we can talk some more when you return from Russia.
Alex	Thanks for coming, Professor.
Hans	*[Quietly to **Huber**]* I'd like that very much.
Huber	Everybody take care of yourselves this summer. I want some decent students in amongst all the Nazis this autumn.
Willi	Don't worry. We'll be there.
Traute	I'll show you out. The catch on the door can be tricky.
Sophie	Bye Herta. Christoph.
Herta	See you.
Christoph	Bye. *[he waits a moment until **Herta** has followed **Huber** and **Traute** off]* I'll be in contact as soon as you get back. I've had some ideas. Maybe I'll jot them down. *[he hurries off]*
Willi	Bye.
Sophie	*[Comes to **Hans**]* What were you whispering with Huber about?

Alex	You both looked very furtive.
Hans	I'm not sure. Perhaps he was a little drunk.
Willi	Old Huber? Surely not?
Hans	If he wasn't ... maybe the White Rose will grow another bloom when we come back.

● ●

SCENE 8

Late July 1942. The atrium at Munich University.

Schmid comes on and notices the graffiti.

Schmid	*[To himself]* Damned subversives!

He covers the graffiti – perhaps with a swastika – then goes off.

● ●

SCENE 9

August 1942. Poland, by a railway line; and the open area.

The Chorus and the Voice of Radio come on.

Chorus	Attention! Attention! Please stand by.
VoR	9th August 1942. Our eastern armies have taken great steps towards controlling the Russian oilfields. The summer campaign moves from success to success. The enemy cannot resist for much longer. Heil Hitler!

The Chorus and the Voice of Radio stay onstage as Hans and Alex come on. They are both now wearing army greatcoats and caps.

Alex	How long have we got, Hans?
Hans	The Captain said five minutes. It's the train's last stop in Poland. Then straight on to Russia.
Alex	It feels so strange going back like this.
Hans	Because of your mother?

Alex	I was four before my father brought me to Germany. Now I'm returning to my birthplace as part of a conquering rabble.
Hans	You mustn't think like that. We can't possibly win the war.
Alex	No? Haven't you had your eyes open? The swastika's flying everywhere we pass through.
Hans	It . . . *we* must be defeated.
Alex	How? Who's going to stop us? Did you hear what the infantry captain was saying on the train?
Hans	*[Disgusted]* Yes!
Alex	Even when they surrender, we kill the communist officials here. It's cold-blooded murder.
Hans	I know.
Alex	Then how can we be defeated? We've become so inhuman, no one can stand up to us.
Hans	*[Takes Alex by the shoulders]* Don't let it drive you mad. Our job is to patch up broken bodies. Not kill anyone. When we go back to Germany, we'll start the real fight again. *[Alex pulls away and shrugs; Hans takes out a bar of chocolate]* Here. Cheer yourself up. I don't like chocolate.
Alex	Ssh!

Hans and Alex watch as the Supervisor comes on with a group of women prisoners, who are carrying picks and shovels. One prisoner, with a yellow star of David on her prison uniform, struggles to keep up with the rest.

Supervisor	Come on! We've got to get the track ready for new sleepers.

The prisoners start using their picks and shovels. The Jewish prisoner struggles to use her pick.

	Hey you! Jewess! Put your back into it.
Jewish prisoner	I'm sorry . . . I was sick when they gave out food yesterday. I haven't eaten for a long time.

| Supervisor | And you won't eat this evening if you don't start working. Now! |

*Hans walks towards the **Jewish prisoner**. He holds out the bar of chocolate towards her. She looks at his uniform and backs away. He puts the chocolate on the ground in front of her.*

Hans	Chocolate. Please take it.
Supervisor	*[To **Hans**]* Hey! What do you think you're doing?
Hans	*[Points to his stripes]* Do you want to argue with a sergeant?

*The **Supervisor** shrugs and turns away, encouraging the other prisoners to work harder.*

*[To the **Jewish prisoner**] Please.*

*The **Jewish prisoner** very deliberately spits on the chocolate.*

Hans looks thoughtfully at her for a moment, then walks over to a clump of wild flowers. He picks one, goes back, and places it on top of the chocolate.

I hoped you might like it. That's all.

The train builds up steam offstage.

| Alex | Hans. The train. |
| Hans | All right. |

*He rejoins **Alex**. As they are about to go off, **Hans** looks back. The **Jewish prisoner** bends down to take the chocolate and the flower. She briefly nods at him.*

***Alex** and **Hans** go off.*

Supervisor   Work!

*The prisoners resume work for a moment, before going off with the **Supervisor**.*

● ●

SCENE 10

August 1942. The living-room at the Scholls' house; and the open area.

*In the living-room, **Magdalene** comforts a weeping **Inge**.*

Chorus   Attention! Attention! Please stand by.

VoR   21st August 1942. Early this morning, our infantry crossed the River Don. There have been light casualties, but expect good news soon. Stalingrad is within our grasp. Heil Hitler!

Magdalene   I'm so sorry Inge. First, father is imprisoned . . . Now this.

Inge   *[Takes a deep breath to control her tears]* As soon as Mrs Reden said 'We've had a visit', I knew what had happened.

Magdalene   They're knocking on so many doors now.

Inge   He was so kind. So loving. *[she starts crying silently again]*

***Magdalene** hugs **Inge** as **Sophie** comes in.*

Sophie   *[Cheerfully]* Finally the foreman's allowed us a day off. *[sees **Inge**]* What's happened? Not Werner? Or Hans?

Magdalene   *[Shakes her head]* Not our boys. Ernst.

Sophie   No? Oh no! *[hugs **Inge**]* Your dear, sweet boyfriend!

Inge   They told Mrs Reden last night. The first thing she saw when she opened the door was the eagle.

Magdalene	*[To Sophie]* You know? The spreadwing eagle on the jacket.
Inge	Straight away she knew. There's only one type of news Nazi officials bring.
Sophie	How was Ernst killed?
Magdalene	In action. That's all the man said. *[shrugs despairingly]* One more life lost in Russia. It doesn't matter to them.
Inge	What about Hans and Werner? What if they're next?
Sophie	Please God, no.
Magdalene	It would kill your father if anything happened to them.
Inge	The only thing keeping him alive in prison is the thought of being with us again. All of us.
Magdalene	Every time I hear footsteps on the street, my heart stops. I keep expecting an eagle.
Inge	Poor Ernst. He was so gentle. He made me laugh. *[cries again]*
Sophie	*[Cold, intense anger]* This must be stopped!

Magdalene, Sophie and Inge go off.

• •

SCENE 11

October 1942. A casualty clearing station in Russia; and the open area.

Werner, in a dishevelled uniform, comes on, trying to shave in a broken hand-mirror.

| Chorus | Attention! Attention! Please stand by. |
| VoR | October 1942. Stalingrad is all but taken. The final pockets of resistance are being scythed down like the last of the corn. Victory is as good as ours. Heil Hitler! |

The Chorus and the Voice of Radio go off.

Hans, in uniform, comes on.

Hans	Werner! You got the message I was coming again?
Werner	*[Trying to be cheerful, although in a deep depression]* Good to see you.
Hans	We're lucky to be stationed so close to each other. I rode over this time.
Werner	*[Wiping off shaving foam with a towel]* How did you get hold of a horse?
Hans	A peasant family sold it to our company. *[points offstage]* Your colleagues are admiring it now. Want to see?
Werner	Maybe later.
Hans	Riding through the grass was wonderful. In some places, it comes right up to the saddle. Miles and miles of it. *[looks round]* I felt I was somewhere different. At sea.
Werner	Any news from home?
Hans	Nothing you haven't heard. Inge's still in despair about Ernst. Sophie hates her war work. You know things are looking a little better for father?
Werner	No?
Hans	Mother says it's possible his sentence will be cut short.
Werner	Why?
Hans	There's a real shortage of financial skills back home. They may release him soon.
Werner	That'd be good.
Hans	And how are things with you?
Werner	The same.
Hans	Really?
Werner	There are still plenty of casualties coming in. The doctors separate the living from the dead. Us ordinary soldiers try to protect the living.

Hans	You don't sound very . . . *[trails off]* You're not ill, are you, Werner?
Werner	No.
Hans	Not even 'Russian fever'? You know? The sky. The countryside. Everything's so vast, it makes you feel small. My mood keeps changing every five minutes.
Werner	My mood doesn't change at all.
Hans	You won't be here for ever, eh? *[beat]* This'll be my last visit. They're sending my unit back next week.
Werner	I wish I was a medical student.
Hans	You'll get leave soon.
Werner	Perhaps.
Hans	Come on, Werner! This isn't like you. You're my crazy little brother. Always joking. Haven't you got a joke for me now?
Werner	No.
Hans	*[Beat]* Mother will ask how you are.
Werner	Don't tell her about the bodies. Don't tell her I stumbled over an arm before breakfast. Don't let her know we're falling apart faster than we can bury the pieces.
Hans	*[Claps **Werner** on the shoulder]* You'll be all right.
Werner	Say that I'm happy and well.
	Werner and Hans look at each other for a moment, then go off.

SCENE 12

22 February 1943. The open area.

Reichhart comes on and sits down casually. The Assistant follows, with a pencil and notepad.

Reichhart	Jacket. Tie. Hat.

Assistant	*[Ticking in notepad]* Yes. Yes. Yes.
Reichhart	Gloves.
Assistant	*[Takes a pair from pocket]* Here you are, Johann.
Reichhart	*[Takes gloves and puts them on]* And, of course, oil?
Assistant	Oil?
Reichhart	Oil! Nothing's more important than oil. Don't you understand that?
Assistant	Of course, Johann. Oil's very important. That's why the Führer tried to capture the oilfields at the same time as Stalingrad.
Reichhart	You idiot!
Assistant	It's true! Some people say that splitting our forces led to the catastrophe that followed.
Reichhart	*[Jumps up threateningly]* Not oil in Russia! Here! Have you got the little can of oil?
Assistant	*[Finally understands]* Oh.
Reichhart	So that everything runs smoothly if we're asked to perform? There must be no catches.
Assistant	There won't be, Johann. I'll see to it now.
Reichhart	Well hurry! And listen! Never use the word 'catastrophe' again.
Assistant	Sorry, Johann.
Reichhart	You could lose your life.
Assistant	I've forgotten the word even exists. Everything's going wonderfully well.
Reichhart	That's better. There's too much defeatist talk around. *[angrily]* And some of it had its roots in that damned studio! When the White Rose gathered again that autumn, it decided to spread its poison right through Europe. Who did they think they were?

December 1942. Eickemeyer's basement.

Traute and **Willi** are putting the last of a batch of leaflets into a rucksack. **Alex, Hans** and **Sophie** are covering the duplicating machine and putting away any other signs of printing, such as stencils and bottles of ink.

Willi	*[Fastening rucksack]* I'm ready.
Sophie	What time's your train?
Willi	Quarter past.
Hans	No need to go yet.
Willi	I don't like hanging around.
Alex	Best not to get to the station too early. The police are always checking bags for black-market goods.
Traute	You should get there just before the train goes out.
Willi	OK.
Hans	Good. That gives me a couple of minutes ... *[Addressing the whole group]* Remember what we said when we got together again after Russia?
Traute	You guys were so depressed.
Sophie	*[Quoting with comic exaggeration]* 'What good's a few hundred leaflets against an entire war machine?'
Hans	We didn't sound like that!
Sophie	You did.
Alex	At least we snapped out of it. We decided to spread our message right through Germany.
Hans	And beyond.
Willi	*[Tapping rucksack]* I wish I was taking these to the Riviera, not just Cologne and Bonn.

Hans	We can do better still in future.
Traute	How?
Hans	You know when our father came out of prison?
Traute	Yes.
Sophie	We saw someone else when we visited him.
Hans	One of his friends. A businessman. And a good sort. That's all you need to know. I explained what we're doing. How a small revolution is starting at this university. But I told him, we're being held back by only having a feeble duplicator. Sophie – a treasurer's report please.
Sophie	He gave us five hundred marks to buy a new machine.
	Willi whistles with appreciation.
Hans	Alex. Would you be able –
Alex	Sure. For that kind of money, I can find something much better. We'll have to pay over the odds. But still . . .
Hans	We need to start printing thousands, not hundreds of leaflets.
Traute	I've got friends in Hamburg who think they can get their own machine.
Sophie	And Hans has been making contact with people who feel like us in Austria. And Italy.
Willi	I wondered why you disappeared for a few days.
Alex	*[Excited]* If we can build up a real network, right through Europe –
Hans	*[Over]* That's the idea. Which is why the new leaflet is headed 'From the Resistance', not 'From the White Rose'. It's not just us, any more. We're going to be part of something much bigger.
Willi	That's excellent! I'm sure my friends in Stuttgart will help.
Sophie	We've got to involve everyone we can . . . Everyone who can afford to take a risk, that is.

ACT 2 SCENE 13

93

Alex	Christoph was asking to help again.
Hans	No. It's too dangerous. Especially now. There's something else you should all know.
Traute	What?
Hans	While Sophie and I were away, we met someone we used to go to school with.
Sophie	You know last year someone delivered a sermon to our parents' house?
Alex	Yes.
Sophie	Later we found this boy had done it. Hans Hirzel.
Hans	Hans knows someone with a contact in the Gestapo. It seems the secret police are going mad now our leaflets are appearing again. Fortunately, they don't know who's responsible. But Hans says they've started taking a lot more interest.
Sophie	And if we begin producing thousands, not hundreds of leaflets, they're going to be really annoyed.
Willi	Excellent.
Hans	*[Angrily]* It's not a game, Willi!
Willi	*[Coldly]* I know that.
Hans	*[Beat]* Sorry. Perhaps it's not the best thing to tell you, just before your journey.
Willi	Don't worry. I'll manage. *[picks up rucksack, ready to go]*
Traute	I'm coming to the station with you.
Willi	No need.
Traute	If I give the police a nice big smile, maybe they won't bother you. *[she demonstrates her smile]*
Willi	Good point.
Traute	Come on.

Hans	Good luck, Willi.
Sophie	See you in a few days.
Willi	I'll bring back some Cologne beer.
Alex	Bye. *[**Willi** and **Traute** go off; to **Hans**]* I didn't know you had contacts with the Gestapo.
Hans	It's not a close contact. But we need to keep our ears open.
Alex	I know we're worrying the Nazis. Have you heard what they're doing for the University's anniversary celebration?
Sophie	*[Joking]* Making us goose-step into lectures?
Alex	They're sending the Governor of Munich and Bavaria to give us a talk.
Hans	That little Nazi, Giesler's coming here?
Alex	That's what Professor Huber says. The authorities are disgusted by the lack of enthusiasm for the war amongst the students. They think the leaflets are partly to blame.
Sophie	That's a real compliment.
Alex	So Giesler's going to give us a pep-talk. *[sarcastically]* Do you think he'll change our minds?

*Alex, **Sophie** and **Hans** stay on and become part of the crowd in:*

● ●

SCENE 14

13 January 1942. The atrium at Munich University.

*Governor Giesler, flanked by some **S.S. Guards**, comes on and stands on the stairway to give his address. **Schmid** stands to one side, watching as **students** and **tutors**, including **Professor Huber**, come on stage and take up positions to listen. Some of the students are in army uniform, and one or two have crutches or other signs of war-wounds.*

Giesler	I find it incredible – absolutely incredible – that while the Fatherland is engaged in the most important struggle of its

existence, some of you students try to hide, with your noses stuck in a book. *[looks at the students in uniform]* I know that others are only too happy to serve in the armed services. I honour you for it. How angry you must be that, here in Munich, and in other places, treacherous anti-war writing is being passed from hand to hand by traitorous scum! It will not be tolerated! Every young man who is fit, should be fighting for his country, not scribbling essays. Or worse! And, girls. What can you do for the Fatherland? That's easy. The best thing, of course, is not to worry too much about your studies. Concentrate instead on providing babies for the Führer. One a year. It's a perfectly natural process. *[some of the students hiss softly]* What better foundation for our thousand-year Reich? Looking round, I can see some of you girls may have trouble attracting a mate. *[speaking as though he's making a great joke]* How shall I put it? You're a little homely-looking. *[more students start hissing]* Never mind girls. If no one else will have you, I offer the services of my assistants. *[he indicates the **S.S. Guards**]* They come from pure bloodlines and will be quite willing to do their duty. I can guarantee you an enjoyable experience. *[the students whistle and boo loudly; some female students get up and leave in disgust]* What do you think you're doing? I'm speaking on behalf of the Führer. Stop it! *[points out some of the noisiest protestors]* They're the ring-leaders. Arrest them!

*The **S.S. Guards** pulls out their pistols and go into the crowd to arrest two **students**. The others back away, but continue booing.*

Schmid   Stop it immediately!

Giesler   *[To **Schmid**]* This is an outrage! *[going off]* The university hasn't heard the last of this.

Schmid   I'm sorry, Governor Giesler. I apologize.

*The **S.S. Guards** take their prisoners off stage.*

Student   *[Calls]* Follow them! Onto the street!

Huber stops Hans from going off. He waits until the stage is empty before he speaks.

Huber	Perhaps it's better if you don't get involved. *[looks over his shoulders before continuing]* You and your friends are having quite an effect.
Hans	This was nothing to do with us.
Huber	Perhaps not the demonstration itself. But your leaflets have shown that protest is possible.
Hans	*[Innocent]* Leaflets?
Huber	Hans, we almost had an understanding before you went to Russia. You and your friends are the White Rose, aren't you?
Hans	*[Beat]* Yes.
Huber	*[Puts out his hand]* I'm proud to have such a student.
Hans	*[Shakes hands]* It's not just me.
Huber	I want to help. When there are no legal means to protest, one has to choose other ways.
Hans	*[Beat, then nods]* All right. We're preparing a new appeal to the whole of Germany and beyond. We'd value your advice on what to say.
Huber	I have some free time now.

*Huber and Hans go off, as a group of **students** come on, with their arms linked. They stop and stand in a line.*

Students	*[Chanting]* Free our comrades! Let them go! Free our comrades! Let them go!

*A group of **Riot Police**, armed with long batons, come on. They begin to beat their batons against the ground. The harder they beat, the quieter the **students'** chant becomes, until finally the **students** are completely silent.*

*Blackout. The **Riot Police** and **students** go off.*

SCENE 15

February 1943. Eickemeyer's basement.

*There is a roll of muffled drums in the darkness. When the lights come up, **Hans** is in the studio, carefully filling a large suitcase with leaflets.*

*The **Chorus** and the **Voice of Radio** address the audience.*

Chorus   Attention! Attention! Please stand by.

VoR   3rd February 1943. It is with great sadness we report that the heroic battle for Stalingrad came to an end yesterday. The efforts of our glorious Sixth Army will go down in history. Finally they have been defeated by a superior force and unfavourable circumstances. Three hundred thousand of our finest men have given their lives for the greater glory of the Fatherland. Future generations will say that the foundations of the German Empire were laid here, in the blood and sacrifice of Stalingrad. Our leader has proclaimed four days of national mourning. Heil Hitler!

*A sombre piece of music plays as the **Chorus** and the **Voice of Radio** go off.*

*The music fades out and **Sophie** comes on.*

Sophie	She's still quite ill.
Hans	Herta?
Sophie	She can't shake off the fever. The baby's growing a little stronger though.
Hans	Herta's tough. She'll pull through. *[keeps filling case]*
Sophie	That's an awful lot of leaflets.
Hans	Alex and I worked right through the night.
Sophie	You've got to get some sleep, Hans. You'll burn out.
Hans	*[Stops filling case]* Hans Hirzel sent a message yesterday.
Sophie	Something bad?
Hans	He says, since the trouble with Governor Giesler, the Gestapo have been going crazy.
Sophie	No wonder. Demonstrations on the street. It's unheard of . . .
Hans	Extra officers have been assigned to find out what's happening in Munich. And Hans says they're very pleased with themselves.
Sophie	Why?
Hans	They think they're close to uncovering the 'White Rose'.
Sophie	*[Shocked]* Oh, no!
Hans	I don't know if it's true. But sometimes, I have the sense we're being watched.
Sophie	Really?
Hans	Once or twice, I've looked over my shoulder. Seen someone scuttling away. Or there's been someone standing opposite the apartment for hours.

Sophie	What do we do, Hans? *[looks round]* Stop printing and destroy all this?
Hans	Then the Nazis have won. They've silenced us, like everyone else.
Sophie	We can't betray Ernst and all the rest who've died.
Hans	I thought about . . . maybe getting out. Going to Switzerland.
Sophie	You could use your army papers.
Hans	Both of us could go. But if we did, they'd only arrest everyone else. And mother and father.
Sophie	They'd make Inge and Werner suffer too.
Hans	So that's not possible.
Sophie	We can't stop what we're doing. We can't run away. What do we do, Hans?
Hans	Keep going. Even if it means risking prison or a concentration camp. As long as we're still alive when the Nazis are defeated, it doesn't matter.
Sophie	Perhaps they don't really know about us yet.
Hans	Maybe the war will end before they find out.
Sophie	After Stalingrad you hear grumbles everywhere. Even from the 'Hundred and fifty per centers'.
Hans	It's like the country's covered in firewood. Especially amongst students.
Sophie	If we can set Munich alight, universities all over Germany'll burst into flames.
Hans	That's what we've got to do, Sophie. *[puts more leaflets in the case]*
Sophie	*[Excitedly helps him]* 'We are your bad conscience. We will not be silent.'
Hans	'The White Rose will not leave you in peace.'

Hans closes the suitcase and brings it with him, as he and Sophie go off.

● ●

SCENE 16

18 February 1943. The atrium at Munich University.

Students come on in groups to go to their next lectures. Schmid bustles across, exchanging Nazi salutes with some of the students before going off.
Traute, Willi and Christoph come on together.

Christoph	I don't like to leave her for long, but I had to see one of my tutors.
Traute	Give Herta our love.
Willi	Tell her to get well soon. *[to Traute]* Now, we'd better hurry if we're going to get to Professor Bumke's lecture.
Traute	*[To Christoph]* Everyone's meeting for lunch at one.
Christoph	I'll have gone home by then.
Willi	*[Calling offstage]* Hans! Sophie! See you at the Bodega.

Hans, carrying the suitcase, and Sophie come on.

Traute	*[Calls]* One o'clock. We've got to fly. *[goes off with Willi]*
Sophie	*[Calls]* Hello and goodbye.

The other students start to drift off gradually under:

Hans	Christoph! How's your new little girl?
Christoph	*[Moving over to Hans and Sophie]* Noisy. Cries all night. *[takes out a sheet of paper and looks over his shoulder]* And I've a little delivery of my own to make. *[gives the paper to Hans]*
Hans	What's this?
Christoph	Read it later. *[Hans puts the sheet of paper in his pocket]* I've done what I said. Jotted some ideas down. It's the outline of a new leaflet. It calls for the end of National Socialism and

demands that men of vision, like Roosevelt, guide the world in future.

Sophie	Sounds interesting.
Christoph	See what you think. Sorry I can't stay to discuss it.
Sophie	Give Herta our love.
Christoph	*[Going off]* Will do.
Hans	*[Tapping pocket]* Thanks, Christoph.

Christoph goes off. Hans and Sophie look round, to see that there's no one watching.

Sophie	Let's do it before the next changeover.
Hans	We'll put some outside every lecture hall.
Sophie	No. Let's put them where everyone can see them. *[she takes the case from Hans and starts going upstairs]*
Hans	*[Following]* What are you doing?
Sophie	*[Going upstairs]* Getting the university to burst into flames. *[at the top of the staircase she opens the suitcase and throws handfuls of leaflets down into the atrium]*
Hans	Yes!

He grabs some leaflets and does the same. When the suitcase is almost empty, Hans and Sophie lift it up and empty the last of the leaflets down into the atrium. They are happy and excited. Hans takes the empty suitcase and starts running downstairs.

Come on.

Sophie follows. As they hurry to go off stage, Schmid steps out in front of them. Hans and Sophie stand still in shock.

Schmid	I've locked the doors. And told the police. I think we should wait in the Principal's room.

Hans and Sophie exchange looks, then follow Schmid off.

*The **Chorus** comes on, gathering all the fallen leaflets as it speaks.*

Chorus (All)	The traitors are found.
Chorus 1	Students. Young students.
Chorus (All)	The traitors are found.
Chorus 2	A brother and sister.
Chorus (All)	The traitors are found.
Chorus 3	Spreading the poison.
Chorus (All)	The traitors are found.
Chorus 4	Challenging Hitler.
Chorus (All)	The traitors are found.
Chorus 5	Calling for freedom.
Chorus (All)	The traitors are found.
Chorus 6	Saying we're finished.

*The **Chorus** divides vocally into two halves for the rising final calls and responses:*

1st Chorus	The traitors are found.
2nd Chorus	They must be dealt with!
1st Chorus	The traitors are found.
2nd Chorus	They must be dealt with!
1st Chorus	The traitors are found.
2nd Chorus	They must be dealt with!

*The **Chorus** goes off.*

18–20 February 1943. Two interrogation rooms at Police Headquarters in the Wittelsbach Palace, Munich.

Hans *enters with* **Anton Mahler**, *who carries a chair.*
Sophie *enters with* **Robert Mohr**, *who also carries a chair.*

The two detectives put the chairs down, some distance apart, in two separate pools of light, to represent two separate rooms. **Hans** *and* **Sophie** *sit down. The two interrogations then proceed, overlapping slightly with each other.*

Mahler	Show me your army papers.
	Hans *takes out his identity papers and gives them to* **Mahler**.
Mohr	Your student papers, please.
	Sophie *takes out her identity papers and gives them to* **Mohr**.
Mahler	*[Checks papers, then returns them to* **Hans**] They seem to be perfectly in order.
Mohr	*[Checks papers, then returns them to* **Sophie**] Thank you.
Mahler	*[Pointing to sheet of paper in* **Hans's** *pocket]* But what's that?
Hans	Nothing. News about a play or something. I haven't looked at it.
Mahler	Who gave it to you?
Hans	Some boy. I don't know who.
Mahler	May I have it?
Hans	Or perhaps it was one of those leaflets that was lying round. Unpatriotic rubbish. *[he starts to tear it up]*
Mahler	*[Snatches the sheet of paper]* Then it belongs in a rubbish bin. *[going off]* I'll throw it away for you.
Mohr	May I call you 'Sophie', Miss Scholl?
Sophie	Yes.

Mohr	Why did you have a suitcase with you at the university, Sophie?
Sophie	My brother and I were on our way to my parents' house. We were going to collect some clean clothes.
Mohr	I see. And why did caretaker Schmid say that both of you were distributing treasonous literature?
Sophie	It must have been someone else. Students all look the same to him. He can't tell us apart.
Mohr	I'm inclined to agree. Subversives aren't usually so well-spoken. I'd like to let you go.
Sophie	*[Hopeful]* Thank you.
Mohr	But my boss isn't sure yet. There are one or two questions to clear up with your brother first.
Sophie	Where is Hans?
Mohr	In another room. He's being treated very well.
Sophie	He hasn't done anything wrong.
Mohr	You may well be correct. We'll have to see. Shall I get you some coffee while we're waiting? Real coffee?
Sophie	Yes, please.
	Mohr goes off as Mahler rejoins Hans.
Mahler	There's something I must check with you, Hans. While you were being brought here, your apartment was searched.
Hans	*[Sarcastically]* Did I leave dirty socks on the floor?
Mahler	My colleagues were more interested in the stamps. A great many eight-pfennig stamps.
Hans	I have a lot of friends.
Mahler	And you use a lot of envelopes. Rather interesting ones.
Hans	I can't remember what they're like.

Mahler	The same type that's used by the White Rose.
Hans	They're very common. You can get them in any shop.
Mahler	So you *do* know which kind of envelope I'm talking about? Oh. And there was something else.

*Hans falls silent as **Mohr** brings **Sophie** a cup of coffee.*

Sophie	*[Taking coffee]* Thank you.
Mohr	I'm afraid we may not be able to let you go after all.
Sophie	Why not? We've done nothing.
Mohr	Another member of your group's been arrested.
Sophie	I don't know what you mean by 'group'.
Mohr	Yes, you do Sophie. And this gentleman is clearly a part of it.
Mahler	*[To **Hans**]* The sheet of paper you tried to tear up. It's taken time to piece together. But now we can read it.
Mohr	*[To **Sophie**]* It says the most dreadful things about the Führer.
Mahler	It calls him a military fraud.
Mohr	It demands the end of National Socialism.
Mahler	The handwriting matches other, perfectly innocent letters in your apartment.
Mohr	The culprit's been identified and taken into custody.
Mahler	Christoph Probst.
Hans	No!
Sophie	No!
Hans	It's only bad luck he gave me that. He hasn't done anything else.
Sophie	You must let him go.
Hans	He's a family man.
Sophie	His wife's just had their third baby.

Mohr	*[To Sophie]* So if it isn't Christoph –
Mahler	*[To Hans]* – who is responsible for the White Rose leaflets?
Hans	I am!
Sophie	I am!
Hans	Nobody else. Not my sister. Just me.
Sophie	Just me. Let my brother go. I'm the only one to blame.
Mahler	*[To Hans]* I'm glad you've decided to start telling the truth.
Mohr	*[To Sophie]* But let's start right at the beginning –
Mahler	We want to know everything about the White Rose.
	Blackout.

● ●

SCENE 18

The morning of 22 February 1943. A courtroom in the Munich Palace of Justice.

Reichhart, now perfectly dressed, comes on with the Assistant.

Reichhart	Yes, it's been confirmed. I'm performing this evening.
Assistant	Wonderful, Johann. And yet . . .
Reichhart	What?
Assistant	Proceedings haven't started yet. So how do you know we'll be needed?
Reichhart	The most important judge in Berlin has been flown in to take charge. The verdict's obviously already been decided. *[looks offstage]* Ssh!

Reichhart and the Assistant stand to one side of the stage, as Police bring on Hans, Sophie and Christoph.
The Clerk of the Court, the Defence Lawyer and the Prosecution Lawyer come on and take up positions.
A crowd of on-lookers comes on, and sits down.

*The Chief Justice, **Roland Freisler**, comes on, wearing a scarlet robe.*

Freisler	*[Passing **Reichhart**]* Everything ready, Johann?
Reichhart	It certainly is, Chief Justice.

Freisler takes his place.

Clerk	The court is called to order.
Freisler	Read the charges.
Clerk	*[Reading from legal document]* Hans Scholl, Sophie Scholl and Christoph Probst are charged with conspiracy, giving help to the enemy and weakening the will of the German people.
Freisler	Filthy, traitorous scum! They deserve eternal damnation for their treachery! *[regains control of himself]* It's a formality, but what does the prosecution have to say?
Prosecutor	There are many witnesses to their treachery, including Caretaker Schmid. However, since the accused have admitted their guilt, we do not propose to call them.
Freisler	Quite right. These criminals have wasted enough of our time. And what of the defence?
Defence Lawyer	Let justice be done. That's all I can say.
Freisler	Well, then. Unless the accused have anything to say themselves –
Sophie	I have, your honour.
Freisler	*[Irritated]* Go on. Quickly.
Sophie	We are called traitors, but all we've done is tell the truth. The war is lost –

Some of the crowd boo and hiss.

Crowd Member 1	Shut up!
Sophie	Why don't you have the courage to face it?

Freisler	*[Interrupting]* Can you say anything to disprove the charges against you, Miss Scholl?
Sophie	No.
Freisler	Then remain silent. Mr Probst? Do you have anything to say in your defence?
Christoph	I thought very hard before writing what I did. I am convinced that ending the war is for Germany's good –
	Some of the crowd hiss.
	[Trying to make himself heard] We mustn't suffer any more Stalingrads. I have three young children and I don't want them to grow up in a country where –
Freisler	Silence! The court doesn't exist to give cowardice a voice. Be silent, Mr Probst. And what of you, Mr Scholl?
Hans	I only ask the court to remember that Christoph has a wife and children. He wasn't involved in printing or distributing –
Freisler	*[Over]* If you're not talking for yourself, don't say anything. *[looks round court]* Well, my task is very easy –
	Robert and Magdalene burst in, with a Policeman trying to hold them back.
Robert	Stop! I want to represent my children.
Freisler	*[To Clerk]* What's happening?
Clerk	The parents of the Scholls, I believe. The father is a well-known trouble-maker.
Robert	*[Going towards Freisler]* I'm here to defend my son and daughter.
Freisler	*[To Policemen]* Throw him out.
	Two Policemen take hold of Robert and drag him away.
Robert	Let me speak! *[being dragged off]*. One day they'll receive true justice.

Magdalene	*[To **Defence Lawyer**]* What'll happen to them?
	*The **Defence Lawyer** shrugs. Another **Policeman** takes **Magdalene** off.*
Freisler	The court has heard all it needs to hear. It's clear that the accused have called for sabotage in wartime and the overthrow of the National Socialist way of life. All three are to be punished by death. Take them away.
	***Hans**, **Sophie** and **Christoph** are escorted off. **Freisler** leaves the courtroom, followed by everyone else.*

• •

SCENE 19

The afternoon of 22 February 1943. A public room in the Stadelheim prison, Munich. There is a waist-high barrier running through the middle of the room.

*Hans is standing at one side of the barrier. **Robert** and **Magdalene** are standing on the other side. **Prison Guard 1** is waiting discreetly at the back.*

Hans	*[Happily]* You'd make us walk for hours, father. And so fast.
Robert	They were only short, little walks.
Magdalene	Robert, they were children then. Of course the walks seemed long.
Hans	But we loved it. Looking up at the mountains. Trying to keep up with you.
Robert	You've developed a much longer stride than I ever had.
Hans	I regret we ever fell out. It was all my fault –
Robert	*[Over]* No!
Hans	And I'm sorry for any pain I'm causing now.
Magdalene	Apologize for nothing. As soon as your father and I get home, we'll find the best lawyer in Bavaria.
Robert	Even in these god-forsaken times, we can make an appeal.

Hans	*[Knows there's no hope]* Perhaps. But if things don't work out ... Give my love to Werner and Inge. To everyone.
Robert	Of course.
Magdalene	I almost forgot. *[takes out paper bag]* I've brought some cake.
Hans	No thanks. I'm not hungry.
Guard One	*[Approaches]* I'm afraid, if you're going to have time to see your daughter as well ...
Hans	*[Reaches out his hand to **Robert**]* Goodbye father.
Robert	*[Shakes his hand]* Goodbye.
Hans	*[Offers his hand to his mother]* Mother.
	***Magdalene** takes his hand and kisses it.*
Guard 1	Please come along.
	***Hans** goes off with **Prison Guard 1**, as **Prison Guard 2** leads **Sophie** on, then stands discreetly at the back.*
Sophie	*[Cheerfully]* I'm so pleased the governor let you see me.
Robert	At least he had a little humanity.
Magdalene	Are they feeding you properly, Sophie?
Sophie	Very well.
Magdalene	I haven't had much time. *[holds up the paper bag]* It's only some cake.
	***Sophie** glances at the **Guard**, who nods. **Sophie** reaches over the barrier to take it.*
Sophie	That's wonderful. We missed lunch because of the trial.
Magdalene	They've no right to be so thoughtless.
Robert	We're proud of you, Sophie. You and Hans.
Sophie	It's not so bad here. The bed's surprisingly comfortable.
Magdalene	Good.

Sophie	I slept very well last night. Just before I woke up, I dreamed I was going to a christening. I was carrying a baby in a long white dress. Suddenly, a great crack opened in the ground. I just had time to lay the baby on the far side, where it was safe. Then I tumbled into the abyss.
Robert	So the baby survived?
Sophie	Yes. I was so pleased. I'd done what I set out to do.
Magdalene	*[Close to tears]* Oh, but Sophie … What if I never hear you come into the house again?
Sophie	We'll be all right. The war'll be over before they can do anything.
Robert	We're so proud of you.
Sophie	Someone had to make a start.
Guard 2	*[Approaching]* I'd like to give you longer. But I'm afraid the prison runs to a timetable.
Sophie	It's all right. *[she reaches over the barrier to squeeze **Magdalene's** hands lovingly.]* Goodbye.
Magdalene	Remember God.
Sophie	And you … Father. *[she squeezes his hands]*
Guard 2	Now, please.

Sophie turns to go off with **Prison Guard 2**.

Magdalene	*[Calls]* We'll visit in a couple of days.
Robert	*[Calls]* What you and your brother have done will go down in history!

Robert puts his arm round **Magdalene** and they go off together.

SCENE 20

Early evening, 22 February 1943. The execution room at Stadelheim prison.

Reichhart comes on with the Assistant. Together they bring on, or reveal, a guillotine.

Reichhart   [*Admiring guillotine*] Magnificent. Well, I'd better tell the Governor we're ready.

Reichhart goes off. The Assistant gradually becomes aware of the audience for the first time, and shuffles with some embarrassment.

Assistant   [*Directly to the audience*] What? What are you staring at? Me or the guillotine?[*he points to the guillotine*] That's right. That's what we use for executions in National Socialist Germany. Gassing is good enough for others, but for our own people, only the best will do. [*increasingly uncomfortable*] Stop looking at me! Someone has to do the job. Maybe today it seems a little harsh. Everyone in the prison thinks Hans, Christoph and Sophie are good kids. We don't like doing this. Just as we won't like executing Alex, Willi and Kurt Huber when their time comes. But what am I supposed to do? Refuse? Don't be ridiculous. When someone barks orders at you, you obey. Or die. When the war ends, and the Allies ask me and my boss, Johann Reichhart, to execute Nazi war criminals, I'll obey them too. After all, I'm a survivor. Just like you.

Reichhart   [*Coming onstage*] They're bringing them across now.

Prison Guard 1 leads Hans, Sophie and Christoph on in a line, with Prison Guard 2 following.

Sophie   [*Turning hurriedly to Christoph*] We're so sorry, Christoph.

Christoph   Don't be. I'm at peace with myself and God. And, if only he gives Herta and the children the strength to keep going, I won't regret any part of what I've done.

Guard 2   Keep moving!

Guard 1 leads them all off stage.

Hans	*[Going off. Shouts]* Freedom!
Reichhart	Ready?
Assistant	Yes.

Reichhart *lays a single white rose at the base of the guillotine, or a rose is projected onto a screen.*

Sophie	*[Through a microphone offstage, or back-lit behind a screen]* Sometimes, when I look up at the stars, I start laughing. I can't help it. It's the most wonderful feeling. To be part of something so extraordinary as this world.

There is the sound of a guillotine blade falling.
A second white rose is laid at the base of the guillotine.

Christoph	*[Through a microphone offstage, or back-lit through a screen]* I believe everything has a purpose. We're on this earth to move towards good, not evil.

114

There is the sound of a guillotine blade falling.
A third white rose is laid at the base of the guillotine.

Hans   [*Through a microphone offstage, or back-lit through a screen*] A rose opens and blooms. It fills a room with its scent. Even when it fades, you remember what a rose was like. Its beauty lasts a long time.

There is the sound of a guillotine blade falling.

***Reichhart** nods with satisfaction, then goes off. The **Assistant** picks up the head of one of the white roses. He sniffs it, considers putting it in his buttonhole, then throws it aside.*

Assistant   [*Directly to the audience*] Too dangerous.

Blackout.

Activities

ACTIVITIES

THE WHITE ROSE AND THE SWASTIKA

Year 8

KEY STAGE 3 FRAMEWORK OBJECTIVES	RELEVANT ACTIVITIES CHAPTER(S)
Reading	
3 Notemaking formats	Story structure
4 Versatile reading	Tracing themes; Story structure; Comparing forms
5 Trace developments	Tracing themes; Comparing forms
7 Implied and explicit	Tracing themes
8 Transposition	Comparing forms
10 Development of key ideas	Tracing themes; Story structure
11 Compare treatments of the same theme	Comparing forms
13 Interpret a text	Story structure
Speaking and Listening	
1 Evaluate own speaking	Debate: survival or death?
3 Formal presentation	Debate: survival or death?
5 Questions to clarify or refine	Debate: survival or death?
7 Listen for a specific purpose	Debate: survival or death?
9 Evaluate own contributions	Debate: survival or death?
10 Hypothesis and speculation	Story structure; Debate: survival or death?
11 Building on others	Story structure; Debate: survival or death?
12 Varied roles in discussion	Debate: survival or death?
13 Evaluate own drama skills	Improvising a scene
14 Dramatic techniques	Improvising a scene
15 Work in role	Story structure; Improvising a scene
16 Collaborative presentation	Story structure; Improvising a scene
Writing	
1 Effective planning	Writing a persuasive leaflet
2 Anticipate reader reaction	Writing a persuasive leaflet; Comparing forms
5 Narrative commentary	Comparing forms
9 Rework in different forms	Comparing forms
13 Present a case persuasively	Writing a persuasive leaflet
14 Develop an argument	Writing a persuasive leaflet

Year 9

KEY STAGE 3 FRAMEWORK OBJECTIVES	RELEVANT ACTIVITIES CHAPTER(S)
Reading	
1 Information retrieval	Tracing themes; Story structure; Comparing forms
3 Note-making at speed	Tracing themes; Story structure
4 Evaluate information	Comparing forms
7 Compare texts	Comparing forms
10 Interpretations of text	Comparing forms
14 Analyse scenes	Story structure
Speaking and Listening	
1 Evaluate own talk	Debate: survival or death?
2 Standard English	Debate: survival or death?
4 Evaluate own listening skills	Debate: survival or death?
5 Compare points of view	Debate: survival or death?
7 Identify underlying issues	Debate: survival or death?
8 Evaluate own contributions	Debate: survival or death?
9 Considered viewpoint	Debate: survival or death?
10 Group organisation	Debate: survival or death?
11 Evaluate own drama skills	Improvising a scene
12 Drama techniques	Story structure; Improvising a scene
14 Convey character and atmosphere	Story structure; Improvising a scene
15 Critical evaluation	Story structure; Improvising a scene
Writing	
1 Review own writing	Writing a persuasive leaflet
2 Exploratory writing	Writing a persuasive leaflet
4 Presentational devices	Writing a persuasive leaflet
12 Effective presentation of information	Writing a persuasive leaflet
13 Influence audience	Writing a persuasive leaflet

Tracing themes

This play is about dissent (disagreement). It traces the true story of a group of young people living in Nazi Germany, who were brave enough to speak out against the Nazi regime.

The playwright introduces the theme of dissent in Act 1, Scene 1. At first there is just one character – Robert Scholl – who voices his disagreement. He is a lone voice. Then, as the play progresses, more characters come to share his viewpoint, and decide to share their views, despite terrible danger. The theme of dissent becomes the main driving force of the play, as the characters feel increasingly passionate about their cause.

The voice of dissent fans out, from one man to his whole family, then to students in Munich, and then to people in other German cities.

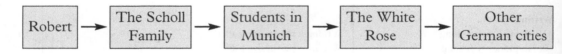

Look closely at how the theme of dissent runs through the play. Copy and complete the grid on page 121, finding examples of how the characters voice their protests and take action. Skim the text, noting possible quotations, before selecting the best for this purpose. Try to find examples in chronological order, showing how the theme develops.

Character	Quotation	How this continues the theme of dissent
Robert	'I'm surprised they don't give you a sheep's head as well.'	Robert is implying that Hans is mindlessly following everyone else, like sheep in a flock, rather than thinking for himself.
Hans		
Sophie		
Christoph		
Huber		
Willi		

'THE PEN IS MIGHTIER THAN THE SWORD'

The White Rose was formed to spread dissent, and to give people confidence to resist the Nazi regime.

1   Why do you think they chose to print and distribute leaflets, rather than stand in the streets and protest?
2   Why do you think they chose to send the leaflets to teachers, priests and pub owners?
3   If you were sending out leaflets to protest against the government today, who might you send them to, for maximum effect?

Fact box

After the death of the White Rose leaders, the text of the final White Rose leaflet was smuggled out of Germany through Scandinavia to England. In the middle of 1943, millions of propaganda copies were dropped over Germany from Allied planes. They were entitled 'The Manifesto of the Students of Munich'.

Story structure

The structure (framework) of this play is based on a series of flashbacks. In Act 1, Scene 2, we see Reichhart and his assistant preparing for an important event, although we are not told what this event is. The history of the White Rose is then told as a series of flashbacks. Eventually, the story is brought up to date, and we realize that Reichhart is preparing for an execution.

With a partner, make a rough sketch to show how the plot is structured, noting the main events. It might look something like this:

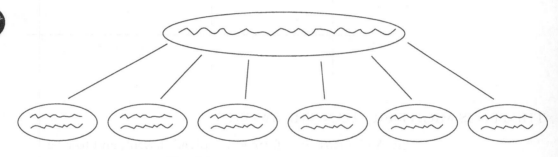

or like this:

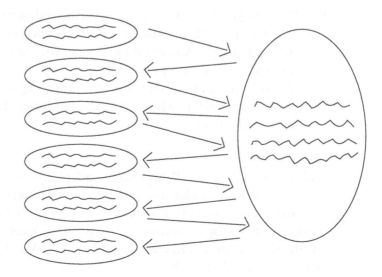

Add labels to your sketch, showing the key episodes.

You could use some of the labels below, sorting them into order.

The trial, February 1943

First arrests, 1938

Students form the White Rose group, 1942

Scholl family at home, 1933/34

Reichhart and his assistant prepare for the execution

Leaflets are printed

Hans in Hitler Youth, 1936

TENSION AND SUSPENSE

The playwright uses Reichhart and his assistant to increase tension and suspense in the play. They are obviously preparing for a formal, important event, but it is not until the end of the play, that we realize what the event is.

1   In pairs, look at the scenes between Reichhart and his assistant. Note down any clues about what event they are preparing for (think about what they are doing, as well as what they say).

2   Reichhart says 'appearance is everything'. How does his concern about his appearance contrast with the main events unfolding in the rest of the play?

3   Choose one scene to act out. Think carefully about the personality of each character and how you will convey this.

4   Rehearse your scene, then present it to another pair, or to the rest of the group.

5   Ask for feedback on your presentation.

Writing a persuasive leaflet

The White Rose group printed leaflets to persuade people to oppose the Nazi regime. Many people already had doubts about it but were too frightened to speak out, knowing that they and their families would be punished. The leaflets tried to reassure people that others thought the same, and to encourage them to take action.

Writers use special techniques when trying to persuade people to act or think in a certain way. For example:

- Repetition – for emphasis
- Emotive language – to get readers emotionally involved in the issue
- Imperatives (commands) – to urge people to action
- Memorable facts or data – to back up the argument
- Rhetorical questions – to address the reader directly and make the issue seem personal to them.

Here are some quotations from the White Rose leaflets. Which of the above techniques do they use?

'Since the conquest of Poland, three hundred thousand Jews have been brutally murdered.'

'The unfamiliar word "freedom" is murmured on every lip, until, on the steps of the temple, we cry out in delight, "Freedom! Freedom!".'

'Every honest German feels ashamed of his government.'

'Use passive resistance to stop the spread of this godless war machine.'

Imagine you are living in Nazi Germany, and have joined the White Rose. You need to work on the next persuasive leaflet with Hans. Plan and draft a leaflet to persuade people to resist the Nazi regime.

1   Read the notes that one member of the White Rose has already jotted down. You might want to use some of the ideas in your leaflet.

- society should protect the weak and disabled, not murder them
- the Gestapo are acting unlawfully
- follow your conscience
- truth cannot be hidden
- 300,000 German soldiers died in the battle of Stalingrad. The Germans lost the battle
- street demonstrations are increasing – join them

2   Think of a short, powerful title for your leaflet.
3   Write in short paragraphs. Make sure each paragraph has one focus.
4   You may wish to research more facts to include in your leaflet.
5   Use the persuasive techniques listed above.
6   Give your rough draft to a partner for their comments.
7   Edit your leaflet to produce a final version. If possible, type your leaflet up on a computer and print out your leaflet.

Debate: survival or death?

In Act 2, Scene 20, Reichhart's assistant addresses the audience directly. He defends his actions, saying: 'What am I supposed to do? Refuse? Don't be ridiculous. When someone barks orders at you, you obey. Or die ... I'm a survivor. Just like you.' He feels he can justify his actions because he is obeying orders.

The members of the White Rose believed that they had to speak out against the Nazi regime, even if it meant death.

Do you think Reichhart's assistant can justify his actions? Hold a class debate on whether people should be punished for obeying orders under threat of death. Follow the steps below.

Step 1
Split into two groups: those in favour of punishing those who have committed crimes, even if they were obeying orders; and those against.

Step 2
Appoint an impartial chairperson, who will have authority to say who can speak when.

Step 3
Each group should appoint a spokesperson to represent their views.

Step 4
Each group should discuss their viewpoint and draw up a list of arguments to support it. They should also try to anticipate what their opponents might say, and think of arguments against them. Some areas to explore when drawing up the arguments are shown in the boxes on page 128. Each group should ensure that:

● everyone has an opportunity to express his or her ideas
● everyone listens to what is said, and responds to it.

Step 5

Each speaker represents his or her viewpoint. He or she might find it useful to have notes to refer to during the presentation.

Step 6

The chairperson 'opens the floor' to other viewpoints – letting everyone have their say.

Step 7

A vote is taken. The side with the most votes wins.

After the debate, think about how you contributed to both the group discussion and the debate itself. Make a note of what you think you did well and what you think you could improve upon next time.

Against punishment	For punishment
● Could an army operate without obedience and discipline?	● Should people make judgements for themselves, or trust 'superiors'?
● Can people be expected to put their family and friends at risk as well as themselves?	● Can you be responsible for something you don't know or understand?
● Does everyone have the ability or knowledge to decide how to act for themselves?	● Are some actions unacceptable whatever the circumstances?
● Is it fair to judge how people act in desperate times?	● Does everyone feel fear in the same way, or are some people naturally braver than others?
● Can anyone be certain how they might act in the same situation?	● Is everyone ultimately responsible for their own actions?

Fact box

Traudl Junge was Hitler's secretary. It was not until the Nuremberg Trials that she became fully aware of Nazi atrocities, but she was excused punishment on account of her youth and ignorance. However, when she found out about Sophie Scholl, who was the same age as her, she realized that she too could have found out about what was really happening, and acted differently.

Improvising a scene

In Act 2, Scene 2 the student friends gather for a picnic in a park. Christoph and Herta share some good news with their friends, but all of them also have serious issues on their minds.

Re-enact the scene as a group.

1   First, allocate parts for Hans, Sophie, Christoph, Herta, Willi, Alex, Traute, a Brownshirt and a Jewish man. Add more friends to the group if you need additional parts.
2   Decide what props you want or whether to improvise them, e.g. picnic rug, basket, string, wine bottle, glasses.
3   Choose whether to stick closely to the script, or whether to improvise the scene. You might wish to alter the scene slightly, for example intervene on the Jewish man's behalf.
4   Each person should prepare for their role by thinking carefully about his or her character. Consider:
    ● approximate age
    ● personality
    ● relationships with others in the group
    ● private thoughts and priorities.
5   Decide what gestures and facial expressions are most appropriate during the scene. Also consider an appropriate tone of voice and physical posture. Remember, you can express lots of things through your body and movements, e.g. tiredness, determination, affection and excitement.
6   Practise your role-playing in pairs before putting the whole scene together. Advise your partner on how to improve his or her character, and ask for comments on your own portrayal.

ACTIVITIES

THE WHITE ROSE AND THE SWASTIKA

While you act out the scene, the teacher may clap his or her hands at any given time, and all the actors have to 'freeze' in their positions. The teacher, or another student, may choose to tap one character on the shoulder, and that character has to say what they are thinking and feeling (in role). Another clap of hands means the scene can continue, until the next 'freeze'.

After acting out the scene, evaluate your own performance individually and as a group. Decide what was successful and what areas you could improve upon.

THE WHITE ROSE AND THE SWASTIKA

Comparing forms

The story of the White Rose has been told in many different ways: through films, plays and historical accounts. Annette Dumbach and Jud Newborn wrote an account of what happened in their book, *Sophie Scholl and The White Rose*. Here is an extract:

Sophie knew nothing about the White Rose and their new campaign. A little over a month after she arrived in Munich, rumours began to circulate that anti-Nazi literature had appeared at the university; reading such a leaflet without reporting it to the Gestapo was a crime. Among the students there was a flurry of tension and excitement; some of them did turn the leaflets in, but most did not.

While attending a lecture, Sophie noticed a mimeographed [copied] sheet lying under a desk; she picked it up. 'Nothing is more unworthy of a cultured people,' she read, 'than to allow itself, without resistance, to be "governed" by an irresponsible ruling clique motivated by the darkest of instincts.' She felt a sudden thrill; darted a look about her. 'The state is never an end in itself. It is important only as a means by which humanity can achieve its goal, which is nothing other than the advancement of man's constructive capabilities.'

Now she saw clearly that there were others at the university who felt as she did; they called themselves *Die Weisse Rose*, 'The White Rose', and they were taking action. But there was something about the words ... She folded the leaflet quickly into her notebook and left for her brother's room, to show it to him.

Hans was not there; she began to leaf through the stack of books on his desk. An old volume of Schiller fell open to a page full of pencil marks: '... if a particular state hinders the progress of the spirit, it is reprehensible and corrosive ... The longer it exists, the more corrosive it becomes.' Turning the pages further, she found the passages cited in the leaflet, word for word, underlined.

She was gripped with shock.

When Hans came in, she confronted him; he denied any involvement, as he already had to Traute Lafrenze. Alex and Christel arrived, and the confrontation became the moment of truth for Sophie Scholl.

Now she was facing her intense and determined older brother, who had crossed the invisible line. Her inner turmoil must have been nearly unbearable. She spoke to Hans about the terrible risks he was taking; she reproached him for adding extra weight to the family's impossible burden: Werner in Russia, their father awaiting a prison sentence, their mother's heart condition deteriorating under the strain. And by now their entire family had at least some sort of Gestapo record.

Hans tried to shrug it off, and his friends defended him. Alex told Sophie that their actions were not reckless, that the choice of people to receive the leaflets was more or less random, and that there was no way to link Hans or Alex to the operation. Christel spoke about acting for a higher good . . .

[Sophie] saw, in spite of her fear, in spite of her terror, that there was no turning back . . . They had crossed over; they had chosen the only way they could. She would now join them.

The same episode is described in the play (Act 1, Scenes 19 and 20). Re-read these scenes carefully. Compare how the different authors tell this part of the story by following the steps below.

Step 1
List the features that are the same in each episode. Think about:

- the characters involved
- what Sophie finds lying around the university
- what Sophie finds in Hans's room
- where she confronts Hans
- Sophie's choice about joining the White Rose
- tension and suspense.

Step 2

List the features that are different in each episode. Think about:

- where Sophie finds the leaflet
- the detail we are given about what is in the leaflet
- the books in Hans's room
- Sophie's immediate reaction when she discovers Hans's involvement
- the different language level.

Step 3

With a partner, talk about why there might be differences between the two accounts. Think carefully about:

- the target audience (age group) for each
- whether it is possible to find out exact facts when the key people involved are dead
- what a narrator can convey in an account, and what an actor can convey through gesture, tone, expression, etc.

WRITING FOR A YOUNGER AUDIENCE

Write a recount of the same episode for a much younger audience. Use the suggestion boxes below to help you.

Use the past tense.

Write just one or two short paragraphs.

Include some direct speech.

Be clear about the sequence (order) of events.

Keep the language simple.

When you have written your first draft, give it to a partner to comment on. Revise the recount, taking into account your partner's comments.

Further activities

1   Use the Internet and other sources to find out more about the White Rose. Write a summary about the group and what they achieved, suitable for an encyclopaedia entry.

2   Choose a character from the play and write a secret diary extract for one day. Record what happened as well as your thoughts and feelings. The day that you record might be in the early part of the play, or the day of the trial and execution.

3   In Act 2, Scene 18 Robert is not allowed to defend his children in court. Improvise a scene where he is. Think carefully about how he might justify their actions to avoid them being sentenced to death.

4   A symbol is a mark or sign with a special meaning. The following symbols could be visible in the staging of this play: a swastika, a star, a white rose. Carry out some research to find out the history of these symbols. What do they represent in the play?

5   With a partner, write a short scene between Sophie and Hans. It could be after their trail but before their execution.

6   Write a short newspaper report about the death of Sophie and Hans Scholl, as it might have appeared in Nazi propaganda. Write a contrasting report as it might have appeared in an English newspaper.